WHERE I LIVE

ALSO BY MAXINE KUMIN

POETRY

Still to Mow

Jack and Other New Poems

Bringing Together: Uncollected Early Poems 1958–1988

The Long Marriage

Selected Poems 1960–1990

Connecting the Dots

Looking for Luck

Nurture

The Long Approach

Our Ground Time Here Will Be Brief

The Retrieval System

House, Bridge, Fountain, Gate

Up Country

The Nightmare Factory

The Privilege

Halfway

WHERE I LIVE

NEW & SELECTED POEMS 1990–2010

Maxine Kumin

W. W. NORTON & COMPANY

NEW YORK • LONDON

Copyright © 2010, 2007, 2005, 2002, 1996, 1992 by Maxine Kumin

All rights reserved

Printed in the United States of America

First Edition

For information about permission to reproduce selections from this book,
write to Permissions, W. W. Norton & Company, Inc.,
500 Fifth Avenue, New York, NY 10110

For information about special discounts for bulk purchases,
please contact W. W. Norton Special Sales at
specialsales@wwnorton.com or 800-233-4830

Manufacturing by Courier Westford
Book design by Chris Welch
Production manager: Julia Druskin

Library of Congress Cataloging-in-Publication Data

Kumin, Maxine, date.
Where I live : new and selected poems, 1990–2010 / Maxine Kumin. —
1st ed.
p. cm.
ISBN 978-0-393-07649-3 (hardcover)
I. Title. II. Title: Looking for luck. III. Title: Connecting the dots.
IV. Title: Long marriage. V. Title: Jack and other new poems.
VI. Title: Still to mow.
PS3521.U638W48 2010
811'.54—dc22

2009040315

W. W. Norton & Company, Inc.
500 Fifth Avenue, New York, N.Y. 10110
www.wwnorton.com

W. W. Norton & Company Ltd.
Castle House, 75/76 Wells Street, London W1T 3QT

1 2 3 4 5 6 7 8 9 0

TO LEE AND JERRY

CONTENTS

LOOKING FOR LUCK

CONNECTING THE DOTS

THE LONG MARRIAGE

JACK AND OTHER NEW POEMS

STILL TO MOW

NEW POEMS

I

WHERE I LIVE

is vertical:
garden, pond, uphill

pasture, run-in shed.
Through pines, Pumpkin Ridge.

Two switchbacks down
church spire, spit of town.

Where I climb I inspect
the peas, cadets erect

in lime-capped rows,
hear hammer blows

as pileateds peck
the rot of shagbark hickories

enlarging last
year's pterodactyl nests.

Granite erratics
humped like bears

dot the outermost pasture
where in tall grass

clots of ovoid scat
butternut-size, milky brown

announce our halfgrown
moose padded past

into the forest
to nibble beech tree sprouts.

Wake-robin trillium
in dapple-shade. Violets,

landlocked seas I swim in.
I used to pick bouquets

for her, framed them
with leaves. *Schmutzige*

she said, holding me close
to scrub my streaky face.

Almost from here I touch
my mother's death.

IN THE MOMENT

Some days the pond
wears a glaze of yellow pollen.

Some days it is clean-swept.
The trout leap up, feasting on insects.

A modest size, it sits
like a soup tureen in a surround of white

pine where Rosie, 14 lbs., some sort
of rescued terrier, part bat

(the ears), part anteater (the nose),
shyly paddles in the shallows

for salamanders, frogs
and little painted turtles. She logged

ten years down south in a kennel, secured
in a crate at night. Her heart murmur

will carry her off, no one can say when.
Meanwhile she is rapt in

the moment, our hearts leap up observing.
Dogs live in the moment, pursuing

that brilliant dragonfly called pleasure.
Only we, sunstruck in this azure

day, must drag along the backpacks
of our past, must peer into the bottom muck

of what's to come, scanning the plot
for words that say another year, or not.

WINTER'S TALE

Even from my study at the back
of the house I can hear an orange drop
upstairs, one of the last to grow

on the dwarf tree you bought me
thirty years ago. When it tried
to overtake the window frame

we cruelly lopped side branches and still
it blossomed and bore its bitter progeny
the size and wrinkle of walnuts.

Repotting, we tore the roots apart,
vermiculite clinging like hatchlings
of silverfish to its tendrils. It thrived,

for years you harvested a pint or more.
But as it aged the fruitage thinned
and hoping to replace it, you soaked

handfuls of seeds. Three consented to sprout.
They shot straight up like pole beans,
greedy underlings sucking in

all the light at the front of the house.
Of course they were sterile.
Today, when I hear an orange drop

I don't let myself think back to the winters
when you'd pick a crop of 20, 30
oranges at once, cut each

one open, force the seeds out, add
enough sugar to make my teeth ache
and boil and boil until the mass

congealed, sheeting off the spoon
in the drear of February while rain
fell on snow making little pockmarks

like mattress buttons in the pasture
outside the steamy kitchen window
and life was bleak and sweet and you

made marmalade.

LORE

In an illustrated text on trees I learn
that the average blue jay collects more than
four thousand acorns over the autumn in
its *expanding esophageal chamber*
but forgets the locus of three out of four,
a figure that saddens me. Still, it accounts
for the tumult of red oak seedlings strewn
along the shady stretch where the pasture ends
and the forest begins.

Who knew the blue jay's beak could open wide
enough to take in the winter's supplies
four at a peck? Still, this falls short
of the chipmunk's stash thanks to its pouch—
four in each cheek and one in the mouth.
But what aspiring Ph.D. kept score
counting acorns all fall and then lay in wait
winter-long for the hungry bird to recall
one out of four of its store
to crack open and eat?

ACROSS THE ESTUARY

The sound of a hammer in the distance
and then the skillsaw singing . . .

silence a little while and then
the hammer recommences

its satisfying thwacks
far, far enough away to soothe.

Let the house be built.
Let its inhabitants be happy.

Let the mourning dove moan
its comforting monody.

I doze in the sun, confident
no one is being nailed to a cross

today or having his arms
chopped off above the elbows.

Not here. Not yet. Safe to say
also not yet across the estuary.

STOPPING

For D.

You were in Paris, I was in Vence
tearing open cartons of Parliaments

I'd stashed a month ago to sustain me,
handing packs out to poets at Fondation Károlyi

and took up killer lozenges of tyrothricin
to repatriate my raw throat, prescriptions

I faked to suck from March till May.
You and your lover toured the Marais

the Louvre, the rive gauche, the Tuileries,
demolishing boxes of chocolate cookies,

dribbling crumbs for the multitude: geese,
pigeons, Gallic Hansels and Gretels.

We stopped. We stopped cold. It was the seventies.
We hadn't met yet, hadn't taken up Scrabble

or tilled a single vegetable.
There we were, as in a dream

in la belle France, impoverished but game
and never, no, never lit up again.

THE WINKING VULVA

When the old broodmare came down with Cushing's, an end-
of-life disease, they took in a friend's

retired gelding, thinking to have a companion
for their own midlife gelding when

the time came to put her down. The mare sprang
into action, newly young,

squatting, crooking and lifting her tail,
squirting urine and winking her vulva, all

classic signs of estrus. Although
bewildered, the newcomer seemed to enjoy

her slavish attention. What old boy
wouldn't? But when in the sweltering

heat her heat persisted, they worried: something
endocrine amiss, an ovarian tumor?

Consulted, the vet only laughed, *good for her!*
At last the inviting vulva gave

up its vigorous winking, the two big guys
lowered their heads side by side to graze.

Between them, regally in charge, the mare
till *yellow leaves do hang* and bid no more.

TAILS

Weekly we tried a different remedy—
mustard, cayenne pepper,
a slurry of garlic and vinegar—
and still the filly nibbled and nibbled
until by spring, when the blackflies came,

strands of horse hair strewed the paddock
mornings, as if ripped loose in combat.
All four of our broodmares
as well as kindly bachelor Jack
she bobtailed up to the dock

like those Stubbs portraits of racehorses
their tails sheared off square—
for some cosmetic ideal or
to make them run faster?
Who can believe we used to do that?

A vital appendage, the tail
arches to say *come closer,* swishes
to say *stand back.* It swats insects.
Clamped, it's a protective shield.
Fanning, it cools body heat.

Old-timey advice: poplar tops.
We bought a cord of lopped-off
skinny boughs and scattered eight or ten
for nightly treats. Sometimes I'd wake
to hear the hollow persistent *thock*

of teeth at work in the dark.
The filly transferred her passion to ribbons
of bark and bobtails grew back. In the spring
we heaved those naked ten-foot rails
into the gully. In May the grass came in.

THE UNFINISHED STORY OF BOOMER

Praise Be
as in *Praise be, it's a filly*

and Hallelujah
as in *Hallelujah, it's another filly*

are middle-aged mares now.
Their dam Boomer is ancient.

She is the daughter of Taboo,
former slave in

a drug scam running
cocaine from Miami

to Boston under
the trailer's floorboards.

When the state
sold her to the slaughterer

we bought her back
for 30 cents a pound and

bred her to a little
Arabian stud with a clubfoot.

33 years later,
Boomer has a metabolic

end-of-life disease.
We'll give her one

last summer on grass,
the vet said cheerfully,

stroking her mane.
Pick out a good place

to dig the hole.
Mid-August.

Boomer is sleek,
gleams like a waxed

Mercedes. Canters
uphill to pasture,

trots down.
I try to imagine

the sweet tasseled fields
without her,

the blind glass of midnight
without her

peremptory whinnies
to summon the others

when lightning
shatters it,

the way
the little herd will

close around her absence,
the way they'll go

on grazing, mouths slobber-
full of the last clover.

THE TASTE OF APPLE

After the year of come-and-go nosebleeds, after
daily washing mucousy blood from his forelegs and flanks
where he swiped himself clean in his impatient horsey way,
I saw the tumor sprout waxy and white
out of one nostril and dangle there, a rare fruit.
Truth rose in my mouth, a drench of gall and wormwood
and I sent for the vet and the backhoe driver
who came together like football coaches conferring.

The vet patted and praised him as she entered the stall
he was born in twenty-six years ago and staggered to his feet
with only a few false lunges in the predawn black and suckled
in small audible gulps from his warm mother. After
she got a line into his neck vein—he jittered a little the way
he'd always pulled back from the needle—
she started the sleep med and I stood with him feeding
him apple slices slowly slowly making them last and when

his head drooped I led him out into the paddock and she shot
the syringe full of pentobarb into his vein. He dropped
with a thud, a slain king, and by then the backhoe had torn
the earth open, the driver deep in the hole raising
icebox-size boulders and deftly arranging them in a row,
scooping red dirt as the late afternoon sun winked out
behind the treeline and after he finished the grave he went
downhill to fit the forks on the front of his machine and by then

I could hardly see as he hoisted the great swaying body aloft
and bore it across the road to the hole and in the cold dark I poured
a libation of apple juice for the earth to welcome his corpse—
some drops spilled on his chestnut flank and some dribbled
on his cheek and splashed onto his yellow teeth as he lay
deep on one side and my hand shook—I could hardly see—
rocking my grief back and forth over this kind death
the taste of apple wasting in his mouth.

THE WHOLE HOG

When you go to your favorite grocery store
and this week's Special is boneless pork
tenderloin that you'll roll in a floured
paste with cracked pepper and rosemary
before you roast it in a hot oven
and serve it with homemade pear chutney

do you visualize up to twenty wet
pink piglets squirming out
of the sow's vagina while she is trapped
in a farrowing crate so narrow that
she can't turn to lick her newborns because
she might roll over and crush one as

they worm their way uphill to a teat
and do you see her being bred back to the boar
only a few days later to make more
piglets and the grown offspring
trucked off to slaughter in
a double-decker tractor trailer, their first

and only time in daylight, the ones
on top shitting and throwing up on the ones
underneath, and the whole glistening mass
of them screaming, before they're forced
down the ramp and into lines
to be killed, the way I heard

and then saw them cross the town
of Storm Lake, Iowa, big corn-fed hogs
bawling, knowing they were going to die,
like those guys beheaded in Iraq?
Well, this is factory farming smack
in the heart of the USA in 2008

so follow your star. *Bon appétit.*

THE LAST ELEPHANT

An umbrella stand upheld by elephant feet
graced the vestibule of my great-aunt Béata
who cherished it as a relic of her palmier
days in Vienna.

I polished its toenails until I read about Murderous
Mary, the circus elephant hoisted by railroad
derrick and hanged in the rain in Tennessee
in 1916 to shame us,

no less barbaric than the poaching of tusks
all over Zimbabwe to feed the black market.
Hides, also meat, waste not want not, even the feet
are put to some use.

Who among us will witness the death of the last
elephant? Presidents and prime ministers alone
or a group of concerned citizens with placards?
Perhaps

like the ivorybill there will be unconfirmed
sightings and distant trumpetings after, but
we're going too, Thomas Hardy's *bell of quittance*
can be *heard in the gloom*.

II

THE VICTORIAN OBSESSION WITH THE PRESERVATION OF HAIR

On the subject of beards, Walt Whitman
wins widest spread. Tolstoy's was
longer but not as full, Marx's
was shapelier, Darwin's
housed butterflies and
Longfellow, where
I meant to
begin,
on-

ly grew his to cloak his scars after
the fire that killed his wife des-
pite his heroic efforts to
smother her flaming
dress by pulling
her into a close
embrace. It
is thought
that

the sealing wax she had been
using to preserve locks
of her daughter's hair
ignited. After that
what came out of
his face every
day was a
memento
mori.

AT THE PITCH

If I could only live at the pitch
that is near madness, Eberhart wrote

but there was his wife Betty hanging onto
his coattails for dear life to the end of her life.

No one intervened when my mother's brother's
wife ran off with the new young rabbi

every woman in the congregation had a crush on.
They rose unleashed, fleeing west

into the sooty sky over Philadelphia
in a pillar of fire, at the pitch that is near madness

touching down in the outskirts of Pittsburgh.
Cleveland. Chicago. O westward!

O fornication! I was sixteen.
Eberhart had written his poem before

he sailed off to World War II and a boy
had just put his tongue in my mouth

which meant he could make
me do anything. No one

holding onto his coattails, no one onto my skirt
until my father switched on the back porch light.

WITH WILLIAM MEREDITH IN BULGARIA

In the grim days of Zhivkov, President for Life,
you and I flew to Sofia in an old Russian Tupelov
where everyone smoked and coughed and spat
and over each window hung a little box marked
in English and Cyrillic *in case of emergency
safety rope.* Laughing, we said *sky hook*, but when
on landing they took away our passports and return
tickets, fear whistled down my throat. You,

ever equable, assured me that as our country's
goodwill ambassadors at the harvest festival
to honor Nikola Vaptsarov, we were safe as sunrise.
Vaptsar, they called him, this war-hero poet
and factory machinist martyred in the Resistance.
Homegrown fascists dispatched him in 1942
but not before he flung the plume of revolution
at them. He survives as a park, boulevard, museum.

They bused us into his beloved mountains
where girls with fruit and flowers offered
ripe pears the size of platters, so succulent
that one bite sluiced our chins. Everyone
in peasant dress, all reds and greens, and endless
speeches. No one mentioned Vaptsarov's life story,
how his countrymen had hung him upside down
for hours and beaten him with rifle butts

before they assembled the firing squad. Because
you were gay and in the closet (this was the seventies)
you leaned your shoulder against mine in public
and squeezed my hand to stay awake through the rhetoric.
Nightly your new artist buddy Misha
hoped to be invited to your college.
Nightly we three drank to this with slivovitz
and Ludmilla, our interpreter, who did not drink,

who once had served for the Lord Mayor of London
and wanted help with amerikanski slang, raised
a dry glass. They took her from us the fourth day.
I said it was because we'd been too friendly.
You disagreed. Misha pulled away and fell silent.
Two more days of speeches, nights of parties
and then the hairpin turns back down the mountains
made queasier by hangovers. *The firing squad.*

And then the worms, Nikola wrote the night before
his execution. *I fell. Someone else will take my place.*
Balkan Airlines' engines throbbed, the door
was latched, we had already fastened our seatbelts
but how could we go? *Sit tight*, you said,
as if we could do anything else. The plane pulsed
angrily. The heavy seal gave way, a functionary galloped
down the aisle restoring our identities, our passports.

CZESLAW MILOSZ VISITS
THE LIBRARY OF CONGRESS

Preceding the poetry reading there is a dinner
to honor the world's most illustrious Polish poet.

I am forced to imagine it since I wasn't invited
and now we're huddled, Czeslaw and I,

backstage in the Green Room, for although
we have never met, I am to introduce him

since I am the Library's Consultant in Poetry
(four years before the new nomenclature, Laureate).

Is there a first prize for awkwardness? Something
immense and inedible? If so we share it.

But somehow we stumble onto the rich improbable
subject of wild mushrooms and now we are

comparing in shared nomenclature *Armillaria mellea*
all piggybacked on one another, their

white spores imitating talcum powder;
Cantherellus cibarius, those golden funnels;

Lycoperdons, little pear-shaped puffballs,
and now he is telling me how he went as a child,

how whole families went with their baskets
to forage all day in the forest plucking

Boletus edulis, digging them one by one
and before we know it we're on.

WATERBOARDING, RESTORED

Carol Houck Smith 1923–2008

Let's take this one out, my editor said,
my wise old editor, who rarely invoked
her privilege, *two years from now*
(it takes that long to go from manuscript
to print) *no one will even remember
the word*. And so I did.

It began:
You're thinking summer, theme parks,
a giant plastic slide turquoise and pink,
water streaming down its sinuous course
and clots of screaming children pouring past
in a state of ecstasy, while you sip gin
and tonic with friends.

Now under the shellac
of euphemism they're calling it
enhanced interrogation.
It follows on the heels of
extraordinary rendition.
Only the mockingbird is cleverer
warbling blithe lies from his tree.

GAME

Before he died
Archduke Franz Ferdinand,
gunned down in Sarajevo
to jump-start World War I,
bragged he had shot three
thousand stags and a miscellany
of foxes, geese, wolves, and boars
driven toward him by beaters,
stout men he ordered to flush
creatures from their cover
into his sights, a tradition
the British aristocracy
carried on, further aped
by rich Americans
from Teddy R. to Ernest H.,
something Supreme
Court Justice Antonin
Scalia, pudgy son of Sicilian
immigrants, indulged in
when, years later, he had
scores of farm-raised birds
beaten from their cages and scared
up for him to shoot down
which brought him an inner joy.
What happened
to him when he was a boy?

THE KENTUCKY DERBY

The Queen stood for what looked
like hours while Barbaro

was honored after they had had
to put him down. *Why*

do they race them so young?
Money. She wore

a lime-green outfit, even
her shoes matched. Her hat

was no surprise to those
of us who remember half

a century of royal millinery.
She displayed a keen eye

for the horses but the announcement
that she rides her horse

on weekends tickled me. Weekends!
Is there so much to do Monday

through Friday when you're
Queen? Dutifully standing

through all the lesser races and taking
the steps without a hand on railings,

that is queenly. But some wicked
Wednesday I'd like to see

Her Majesty, entourage and all
in the saddle.

SYMPOSIUM

Last call for the symposium at 4 p.m.
to examine the works of W. H. Auden
whom I remember always in carpet slippers.

X from Hum. 101 will discuss the early poems,
Y from Eng. 323 will discuss the later poems
in the symposium that opens at 4 p.m.

Spender famously said, *Poor Auden; soon*
we'll have to take off his face and iron it to see who he is.
Perhaps he had bunions, thus the carpet slippers.

Lord Byron, Faustus, Yeats, September 1
1939, these poems should head the list
of works discussed in the symposium at 4 p.m.

which will reaffirm the poet's place in the pantheon:
wittier than Eliot, more readable than Pound,
both too erudite to read in carpet slippers

but knowing how all the instruments can disagree
and cleverest hopes expire, let us revere
his pleated face in the symposium at 4 p.m.
while I revisit him onstage in carpet slippers.

A BRIEF HISTORY OF ENGLISH ROMANTICISM

How chaste was it? Does it matter?
Did ever a poet have such a sister?

It's true that he gave her the ring
to wear all day the day before his wedding

which she didn't attend for fear
of drenching the ceremony with tears.

For seven years she'd had him
to herself, her only William,

without a murmur she'd gone with him
to settle his finances on "Mme Williams"

who'd been his mistress, and the child he'd never seen,
nine-year-old adorable Caroline.

I love that they all bathed together that day,
a make-believe family on the beach at Calais.

And later, the rift with Coleridge, by then a goner—
to think two men who'd been closer than blood brothers

could break up over poetry
and years go by in icy formalities. . . .

Well, two of my brothers died unreconciled
though neither was addicted, merely livid

with rage at the other. At least Will and Sam
closed lovingly despite the wrack of laudanum

and even though *Christabel, Part Two*
never got written and William's few

late poems didn't add much to his oeuvre
nothing could detract from that first creative surge

side by side those months in the Quantock Hills
and I'll never forget how Coleridge walked 40 miles

to meet Wordsworth, the very beginning of this story
that leads us back into the title: A Brief History. . . .

COLERIDGE'S LAUNDRY

I wanted to talk about Coleridge
who was anything but handsome
and was always leaving Sara his wife

to walk amazing distances
for conversations with his pals:
Poole, Lamb, Wordsworth et al.

I said, so what if the Pantisocratic
ideal was just another hippie
utopia where everyone labored by hand

in the morning and studied or wrote
in the afternoon? So what if the project
conceived in poverty went down

in unexpected endowments,
the Lannans and MacArthurs of their day?
I wanted to read about laudanum:

how many drops at bedtime and
did he add them to water or tea
or something stronger.

When I closed my book I fell
asleep as instantly as if I'd downed
50 drops in two fingers of scotch straight up.

In my dream this poem was given
a communion wafer
and a blood transfusion.

I woke with baked cotton on my tongue.
My pulse was vigorous, my heart
was with Sara, the mountain

of laundry, her always absent Coleridge.
Domesticity and migraines,
miles and miles on foot.

CHILDBIRTH, DOVE COTTAGE, THE WORDSWORTHS

In September Basil Montagu
  arrived in Grasmere for a stay
    of more than three weeks,
      accompanied
        by his third wife,
          his second wife
            like his first
              having died in childbirth.
                —Adam Sisman, *The Friendship*

And of course they were mourned
and appropriately interred
and Anna, Wife the Third,
who brought her little namesake
into the union, mercifully remained childless.

Given the odds, I think how willful
she was to take a chance on Basil
whose housekeeper she had become perforce
after her young husband died. Still,
staying single might have been worse.

I weigh it: better to chance a breech birth,
be wrenched apart by amateur surgeons
only to die later of childbed fever, or
to wither penniless, forever
dependent on resentful relatives?

And then I wonder, how did Dove Cottage
accommodate the lot of them—
William and the women
who served him: wife Mary,
sister Dorothy, and after laudanum

had stealthily shrunk the aura
of their friendship, Coleridge's Sara—
that Sara, with his wife's sister Sara, who despised her
as her intellectual inferior.
A houseful of menstruating women

and the cloths they boiled clean, hung to dry.
Four small rooms down, four up,
no running water, an outdoor privy.
Think of the chamber pots.
Also the accumulated children.

Think of the feeding, the scrubbing,
the apportioning of beds. The garden
to be planted, peas and runner beans.
And look who takes on
the worst of it, peeling and peacemaking.

First up, last to bed, Dorothy.
Is it any wonder that the reader aches
for Dorothy, said to be virginal,
her last twenty years invalided, senile,
Dorothy who gave so much and got so little?

LOOKING FOR LUCK

CREDO

I believe in magic. I believe in the rights
of animals to leap out of our skins
as recorded in the Kiowa legend:
Directly there was a bear where the boy had been

as I believe in the resurrected wake-robin,
first wet knob of trillium to knock
in April at the underside of earth's door
in central New Hampshire where bears are

though still denned up at that early greening.
I believe in living on grateful terms
with the earth, with the black crumbles
of ancient manure that sift through my fingers

when I top-dress the garden for winter. I believe
in the wet strings of earthworms aroused out of season
and in the bear, asleep now in the rock cave
where my outermost pasture abuts the forest.

I cede him a swale of chokecherries in August.
I give the sow and her cub as much yardage
as they desire when our paths intersect
as does my horse shifting under me

respectful but not cowed by our encounter.
I believe in the gift of the horse, which is magic,
their deep fear-snorts in play when the wind comes up,
the ballet of nip and jostle, plunge and crow hop.

I trust them to run from me, necks arched in a full
swan's S, tails cocked up over their backs
like plumes on a Cavalier's hat. I trust them
to gallop back, skid to a stop, their nostrils

level with my mouth, asking for my human breath
that they may test its intent, taste the smell of it.
I believe in myself as their sanctuary
and the earth with its summer plumes of carrots,

its clamber of peas, beans, masses of tendrils
as mine. I believe in the acrobatics of boy
into bear, the grace of animals
in my keeping, the thrust to go on.

LOOKING FOR LUCK IN BANGKOK

Often at markets I see
people standing in line
to walk under an elephant.
They count out a few coins,
then crouch to slip beneath
the wrinkly umbrella that smells
of dust and old age
and a thousand miracles.

They unfold on the other side
blessed with long life,
good luck, solace from grief,
unruly children, and certain
liver complaints.

Conspicuous Caucasian,
I stoop to take my turn.
The feet of my elephant are stout
as planted pines. His trunk completes
this honest structure,
this tractable, tusked,
and deeply creased
endangered shelter.

I squat in his aromatic shade
reminded of stale bedclothes,
my mother's pantry shelves
of cloves and vinegar,
as if there were no world of drought,
no parasites, no ivory poachers.
My good luck running in
as his runs out.

PRAISE BE

Eleven months, two weeks in the womb
and this one sticks a foreleg out
frail as a dowel quivering
in the unfamiliar air and then
the other leg, cocked at the knee
at first, then straightening
and here's the head, a big blind fish
thrashing inside its see-through sack
and for a moment the panting mare
desists, lies still as death.

I tear the caul, look into eyes
as innocent, as skittery
as minnows. Three heaves, the shoulders pass.
The hips emerge. Fluid as snakes
the hind legs trail out glistering.
The whole astonished filly, still
attached, draws breath and whinnies
a treble tremolo that leaps
in her mother who nickers a low-key response.

Let them prosper, the dams and their sucklings.
Let nothing inhibit their heedless growing.
Let them raise up on sturdy pasterns
and trot out in light summer rain
onto the long lazy unfenced fields
of heaven.

HAY

Day One: Above the river I hear
the loud fields giving up their gold,
the giant scissors-clack of Ruddy and Ned's
antique machine laying the timothy
and brome in windrows to be tedded,
this fierce anthood that persists
in taking from and giving back to the land,
defying the chrome millennium
that has contempt for smallscale backbreak.

Three emeralds, these interlocked three fields
free-leased for the tending and brushing out,
tidied up every fall like a well-swept
thrifty kitchen, blackberry and sumac
held at bay, gray birch and popple
brought down, the wild cherry lopped,
and gloriously every March
the wide white satin stretch besmirched
with dripping cartloads of manure.

Day Two: Sun bakes the long lines dry.
Late afternoon clouds pile up to stir
the teased-up mass with a southerly breeze
and since the forecast's fair, Ruddy and Ned
relax, play-punch, kidding each other,
calling each other Shirley, a name neither
owns up to, although once Scots-common
enough in New England back when
their patched rig was a modern invention.

Their dogs, four littermates,
Nutmeg, Cinnamon, Allspice and Mace,
Chessies with gums as pink as rubber
erasers and pink-rimmed eyes,
flat irises you can't look into,
their dogs, companionable roughnecks
always riding in the backs of their pickups
or panting, lying under them for shade,
look benignly on their sweating labors.

Day Three: The old baler cobbled from
other parts, repaired last winter,
cussed at in the shed in finger-
splitting cold when rusted bolts
resisted naval jelly, Coca-Cola, and
had to be drilled out in gritty bits,
now thunking like a good eggbeater
kicks the four-foot cubes off
onto the stubble for the pickups

and aggie trucks—that's our three-quarter ton
Dodge '67, slant-six engine
on its third clutch, with a new tie rod,
absent one door handle and an
intermittent taillight—
we'll carry fifty-two bales at a time
if they're pitched up and set on right.
Grunters and haulers, all of us
in these late-August heroics.

Interlude: The summer I was eleven
I boarded on a dairy farm in Pennsylvania.
Mornings we rode the ponies bareback
up through eiderdowns of ground fog,
up through the strong-armed apple orchard
that snatched at us no matter how we ducked,
up to the cows' vasty pasture, hooting and calling
until they assembled in their secret order
and we escorted them down to the milking barn
where each one gravely entered her stanchion.
There was no pushing or shoving.
All was as solemn as Quaker Meeting.

My four were: Lily, Martha, Grace and May.
May had only three tits. I learned to say *tit*
as it is written here. I learned to spend
twenty minutes per cow and five more stripping,
which you do by dipping your fingers in milk
and then flattening the aforementioned tit
again and again between forefinger and thumb
as you slide down it in a firm and soothing motion.
If they don't trust you they won't let down.
They'll get mastitis and their agony will be
forever on your conscience. To this day
I could close my eyes and strip a cow correctly.

I came to love my black and white ladies.
I loved pressing my cheek against each flank
as I milked. I almost came to love cowflops,
crisp at the edges, smelly pancakes.
I got pinkeye that summer, they say
I caught it from the cows, I almost lost the eye.
Meanwhile, we had squirt fights, cow to cow.
We squirted the waiting kittens full.
We drank milk warm from the pail,
thirsty and thoughtless of the mystery
we drank from the cow's dark body,
then filed in for breakfast.

They put up hay loose there, the old way,
forking it into the loft from the wagon rack
while the sweaty horses snorted and switched off flies
and the littlest kids were commanded to trample it flat
in between loads until the entire bay
was alight with its radiant sun-dried manna. . . .
It was paradise up there with dusty sun motes
you could write your name in as they skirled and drifted down.
There were ropes we swung on and dropped from and shinnied up
and the smell of the place was heaven, hurling me back
to some unknown plateau, tears standing up in my eyes
and an ancient hunger in my throat, a hunger. . . .

Perhaps in the last great turn of the wheel
I was some sort of grazing animal.
Perhaps—trundling hay in my own barn
tonight and salivating from the sweetness—
I will be again. . . . When I read Neruda's
we are approaching a great and common tenderness
my mind startles and connects to this
all but obsolete small scene above the river
where unspectacular people secure
their bulky loads and drive away at dusk.

Allegiance to the land is tenderness.
The luck of two good cuttings in this climate.
Now clean down to the alders in the swale,
the fields begin an autumn flush of growth,
the steady work of setting roots, and then
as in a long exhale, go dormant.

SUBDUING THE DREAM IN ALASKA

at the Beaver Dome Correctional Facility

In the visiting poet's workshop
the assignment is to write down a dream.
The intent, before the week is out,
is to show how much a poem is like
a dream set straight, made rational.
A dream scrubbed up and sent to school.

The reedy boy, so withdrawn
day after day he never gets beyond
printing his name in the upper
lefthand corner, is in for rape.

The big man with the jolly laugh
and beer belly is serving time
for incest. Two swaggerers in orange
jumpsuits have records for assault

with a dangerous weapon, which here
translates as knife. An older man,
exposed to his shame as illiterate,
has ninety days for poaching a moose.

He whispers his dream. The poet takes
it down in a lightning scribble
that will be difficult to read back.
There are caribou and snowmobiles in it,

cascades of antlers and a washbucket
of blood upended on the snow.
They say they dream of their ancestors,
the Inuit villages of their great-uncles,
seals whelping their pups on the ice cap,
the sun disappearing at winter solstice,
the treasure of their happy childhood,
the gift of their first flensing knife.

But in truth each night the conqueror comes in.
At a gallop he rides them, building our highway,
scratching up earthworks, laying our pipeline,
uncorking the bottle and smiling betrayal.

THE PATRIOT

Old World *Rattus*
of Norwegian extraction
and dark complexion
enters this poem
a naturalized American,
swims under water
a hundred yards,
slips through a hole
the size of a quarter
and drops fifty feet
onto concrete,
an unruffled bird.
Like the homeless
he lives on discards.
Like them he is
a fact of life in
the metropolis.
Whatever comes down
—bits of bagel,
pizza, sweet roll—
is his.

Shooting him
at the dump
used to be
an honorable sport
for Sunday

in the country.
Men from the mill
would get up from dinner,
take a six-pack
in the pickup,
perch on the hood
and squeeze the trigger
of the .22
whenever something stirred.
Maybe only the toe
of a bread wrapper.
Maybe a kill.
It was comical
the way he used to jump
before the dump
became a landfill.

The year they closed
it down, everyone
with a barn, a horse,
a couple of leghorns,
a scatter of grain
began to catch
sidelong flashes
of that red eye,
that hairless tail.
Poison is touchy.

You had to spy
out the hole.
You had to watch
where the earth
was scratched.
You set the bait.
You learned the patience
of a lover.
You had to bury
his sleek dead body
over and over.
Faithful, robust
Rattus norvegicus
comes back to ghost us
in subway and cellar.
Wherever our roots are
his nest is beside us.
His head in the pail,
our nocturnal zealot,
his teeth in the trough,
ubiquitous patriot,
nothing we leave him
is ever enough.

THE POETS' GARDEN

After the first revolution
the poets were busier than
cabbage moths in the garden.
They praised the new nation,
the rice paddies, the rumps of the peasants
raised skyward as they planted,
the new children who would grow up to be literate,
have electricity, running water,
almost enough to eat.
They praised the factories
that belonged to everyone,
the bolts of black cloth
and the shimmering orange tractors
that ran like heavy-footed dragons
over the earth.

After the counterrevolution
the poets were excommunicated.
They were farmed out as swineherds.
They cleaned privies.
They swept the aisles of factories.
They learned to make light bulbs and fertilizers
and little by little they mastered
the gray art of ambiguity.
Out of the long and complex grasses
of their feelings they learned
to plait meanings into metaphor.
It was heavy weather.

After the next revolution
it rained melancholy, it is still raining
in the poets' garden. But they are planting
and busy white moths flutter
at random along the orderly rows,
a trillion eggs in their ovipositors
waiting to hatch into green loopers
with fearsome jaws.

THE NUNS OF CHILDHOOD: TWO VIEWS

1.

O where are they now, your harridan nuns
who thumped on young heads with a metal thimble
and punished with rulers your upturned palms:

three smacks for failing in long division,
one more to instill the meaning of *humble*.
As the twig is bent, said your harridan nuns.

Once, a visiting bishop, serene
at the close of a Mass through which he had shambled,
smiled upon you with upturned palms.

"Because this is my feast day," he ended,
"you may all have a free afternoon." In the scramble
of whistles and cheers one harridan nun,

fiercest of all the parochial coven,
Sister Pascala, without preamble
raged, "I protest!" and rapping on palms

at random, had bodily to be restrained.
O God's perfect servant is kneeling on brambles
wherever they sent her, your harridan nun,
enthroned as a symbol with upturned palms.

2.

O where are they now, my darling nuns
whose heads were shaved under snowy wimples,
who rustled drily inside their gowns,

disciples of Oxydol, starch and bluing,
their backyard clothesline a pious example?
They have flapped out of sight, my darling nuns.

Seamless as fish, made all of one skin,
their language secret, these gentle vestals
were wedded to Christ inside their gowns.

O Mother Superior Rosarine
on whose lap the privileged visitor lolled
—I at age four with my darling nuns,

with Sister Elizabeth, Sister Ann,
am offered to Jesus, the Jewish child-
next-door, who worships your ample black gown,

your eyebrows, those thick mustachioed twins,
your rimless glasses, your ring of pale gold—
who can have stolen my darling nuns?
Who rustles drily inside my gown?

REMARKABLE WOMEN: AN APOSTROPHE

Beatrix Potter, on the stout side, dressed
"in tweeds thick enough to stop a bullet"
woven from the wool of your own sheep,
looking back across those green fields in
your old age you said, *If I had been
caught young enough I could have become
anything.* I salute what you became

and you, Louisa May, on record claiming
*I was born with a boy's spirit under my bib
and tucker*, working to keep the clan afloat
that Bronson Alcott dreamily left drift,
inventions on a tribe, book after book.
Eight Cousins was my favorite, orphaned Rose
saved from invalidism by Uncle Alec. . . .

and you, Helen Nearing, almost ninety, kneeling
to dig potatoes for a guest's lunch, confessing
*I was twenty-six before I planted so much
as a radish. Oh, I was lily-handed,*
square-knuckled, liver-spotted, laying up
the house you built with Scott stone by stone,
tending the sugarbush, the raised-bed garden,

I salute you all, I take you with me wherever
I go to fire me with your fevers.

THE CHAMBERMAIDS IN THE MARRIOTT
IN MIDMORNING

are having a sort of coffee klatch as they clean
calling across the corridors in their rich contraltos
while luffing fresh sheets in the flickering gloom
of the turgid passionate soaps they follow from room to room.

In Atlanta they are black, young, with eloquent eyes.
In Toledo white, middle-aged, wearing nurses' shoes.
In El Paso always in motion diminutive Chicanas
gesture and lift and trill in liquid Spanish.

Behind my "Do Not Disturb" sign I go wherever they go
sorely tried by their menfolk, their husbands, lovers or sons
who have jobs or have lost them, who drink and run around,
who total their cars and are maimed, or lie idle in traction.

The funerals, weddings and births, the quarrels, the fatal gunshots
happen again and again, inventively reenacted
except that the story is framed by ads and coming attractions,
except that what takes a week in real life took only minutes.

I think how static my life is with its careful speeches and classes
and how I admire the women who daily clean up my messes,
who are never done scrubbing with Rabelaisian vigor
through the Marriott's morning soaps up and down every corridor.

THE CONFIDANTES

Dorothy Harbison, *aetat* 91,
stumps into the barn on her cane and my arm,
invites the filly to nuzzle her face,
her neck and shoulders, her snowdrift hair
and would very likely be standing there
still to be nibbled, never enough
for either of them, so sternly lovestruck
except an impatient middle-aged daughter
waits to carry her mother off.

    In Camden, Maine the liveryman
    at the end of town, a floridly grand
    entrepreneur, sends for Dorothy
    whenever he has a prospect at hand.
    She is nine or ten. Given a knee
    up she can ride any horse on the place.
    If the deal goes through, a 50¢ piece
    pops in her pocket, but Dorothy's pride
    soars like a dirigible, its ropes untied.

It was all horses then, she says,
combing the filly's mane with her fingers,
soothing and kneading with practiced hands
from throatlatch to sensitive poll to withers.
All horses. Heavenly. You understand.

It's the year of the Crash. I'm almost four.
My father is riding a horse for hire
in the manicured parkland at Valley Green.
When he clops into sight the trees take fire,
the sun claps hands, dust motes are becalmed.
They boost me up to his shifting throne—
Whoa, Ebony!—and I put my palms
flat on the twitching satin skin
that smells like old fruit, and memory begins.

Leaving, Dorothy Harbison
speaks to the foal in a lilting croon:
I'll never wash again, I swear.
I'll keep the smell of you in my hair.
and stumps out fiercely young on her cane.

THE RENDEZVOUS

How narrow the bear trail
through the forest,
one paw print following
the other in the manner
of good King Wenceslas
tagged by his faithful serf.

How, according to the legend,
a bear is able to feel shame
and if a woman meets a male bear
she should take off all her clothes,
thereby causing him
to run away.

How I meet a male bear.
How I am careful not
to insult him. I unbutton
my blouse. He takes out
his teeth. I slip off
my skirt. He turns
his back and works his way
out of his pelt,
which he casts to the ground
for a rug.

He smells of honey
and garlic. I am wet
with human fear. How
can he run away, unfurred?
How can I, without my clothes?

How we prepare a new legend.

CONNECTING THE DOTS

LETTERS

"Dear Muzz," I wrote, the summer I was ten
from a seedy nature camp in the Poconos
with cows and calves, huge geese, some half-wild ponies
—heaven for the urban savage I was then—
"I have to do this letter to get breakfast.
Kiss Kerry for me. I milked a cow named Clover."
(Kerry, my dog, already dead, run over
the week I left.) Muzz from the bosomy British
matron in charge of spunky orphans who reclaim
the family's fortunes in a book I adored.
My older brothers called you Dolly, cleared
as almost-adults to use your cute nickname.
"Dear Muzz, with love" however smudged and brief
from your animal, sole daughter in your life.

Your animal, sole daughter in your life,
I mourned my dog, the slaughter of Clover's calf.
You were born Bella, number six of twelve.
The butter was spread too thin, childhood too brief
shared with Eva, Sara, Lena, Esther, Saul,
Meyer, Nathan, Oscar, Dan, Jay, Joe.
The younger ones mewed to be held by you.
The older ones, above your crib, said "doll."
You made me your confessor. At eighteen
you eloped, two virgins fleeing Baltimore,
buttoned in one berth by a Pullman porter
who jollied your tears at breakfast next morning

before the train pulled into Buffalo.
Your face announced Just Married, you blushed so.

Just married, one day pregnant, you blushed so
pink Niagara's fabled sunset paled.
"Papá will kill me when he hears," you quailed
but the first grandchild, a boy, softened the blow.
You told me how your mother had slapped your face
the day your first blood caked along your thighs,
then sent you to your sister for advice.
Luckier, I was given *Marjorie May's*
Twelfth Birthday, a vague tract printed by Kotex,
so vague it led me to believe you bled
that one year only, and chastely left unsaid
the simple diagrammatics about sex.
When was it that I buried Muzz, began
to call you by the name that blazoned Woman?

I came to call you Dolly, The Other Woman,
the one I couldn't be. I was cross-eyed,
clumsy, solitary, breasts undersized.
Made wrong. An orthodontist's dream. A bookworm.
That winter, a houseguest, his wife gone shopping,
pinned me in my bedroom by the mirror
and as we both watched, took out to my horror
a great stiff turkey neck, a hairless thing
he wanted to give me. How could I tell you this,

how he pressed against me, put it in my hand,
groped my nipples, said, "Someday you'll understand"?
How tell you, who couldn't say vagina, penis?
This isn't recovered memory. I never forgot it.
I came to call you Dolly. That's when it started.

At 14, I called you Dolly. The war had started,
absorbing my brothers one by one. The first-
born fought in Rommel's Africa, then crossed
to the Italian Boot. Your cocktail parties
grew shriller that year, the air more fiercely mortal
as the second son went off to ferry bombers
over the Burma Hump. Your hair, by summer,
began to thin, then fell out, purgatorial.
The youngest, apple of your eye, was shot
down in the Pacific, plucked from his atoll
and survived with a pair of shattered ankles.
You had to wear a wig. I dared to gloat.
The rage of adolescence bit me deep.
I loathed your laugh, your scarves, your costly makeup.

Your laugh, your scarves, the gloss of your makeup,
shallow and vain. I wore your lips, your hair,
even the lift of my eyebrows was yours
but nothing of you could please me, bitten so deep
by the fox of scorn. Like you, I married young
but chose animals, wood heat, hard hours

instead of Sheffield silver, freshcut flowers,
your life of privilege and porcelain.
My children came, the rigorous bond of blood.
Little by little our lives pulled up, pulled even.
A sprinkle here and there of approbation:
we both agreed that what I'd birthed was good.
How did I come to soften? How did you?
Goggy is what my little ones called you.

Goggy, they called you, basking in the sun
of your attention. You admired their ballet;
their French; their algebra; their Bach and Debussy.
The day the White House rang you answered, stunned
your poet-daughter was wanted on the phone
—the Carters' party for a hundred bards.
We shopped together for the dress I'd wear.
Our rancors melted as ocean eases stone.
That last year of your life, the names you thought of:
Rogue, Doc, Tudor, Daisy, Garth,
the horses of your lost Virginia youth.
You said them, standing in my barn, for love.
Dying, you scratched this fragment for me, a prize;
"Darling . . . your visit . . . even . . . so brief . . . Muzz."

REHEARSING FOR THE FINAL RECKONING
IN BOSTON

During the Berlioz *Requiem* in Symphony Hall
which takes even longer than extra innings
in big league baseball, this restless Jewish agnostic
waits to be pounced on, jarred by the massed fanfare
of trombones and trumpets assembling now in the second
balcony, left side, right side, and at the rear.

Behind them, pagan gods in their niches
acoustically oversee this most Christian
of orchestrations: the resting Satyr
of Praxiteles, faun with infant Bacchus,
Apollo Belvedere, Athena, Diana
of Versailles with early greyhound.

When the wild mélange cries out
Dies irae, all of our bared hearts pulse
under Ozawa's baton. He is lithe as a cat,
nimble as Nureyev, another expatriate.
But even Ozawa dressed in white sweats
cannot save us up here in peanut heaven, or save

patrons downstairs in the best seats canted back
for the view, who wear the rapt faces of the fifties
tilted to absorb the movie on the 3-D screen.
Naught shall remain unavenged, sings the chorus.
What trembling there shall be when we rise again
to answer at the throne. That's all of us

since Adam, standing on one another's shoulders
three or four deep, I should imagine,
acrobats of the final reckoning.
And what terror awaits those among us
whose moral priorities are unattached
to Yahweh, Allah, Buddha, Christ:

forgiving without praying for forgiveness,
the doing unto others, scrubbing toilets,
curbing lust, not taking luck for granted?
Are the doubters reckoned up or just passed over?
Hector was almost passed over, his *Requiem*
unplayed, save for a general killed in battle. . . .

How should one dress for the Day of Judgment?
At a working rehearsal the chorus is motley,
a newborn *fin de siècle* in T-shirts and jeans.
But what will they wear when the statues have crumbled
in 2094? Brasses and massive tympani close
the *Lacrymosa*. Metallic spittle is hot in my throat.

Now we enter the key of G major, the Lamb
of God key of catharsis and resolution.
Like a Janus head looking backward and forward,
pockmarked by doubt I slip between cymbals
to the other side of the century where our children's
children's children ride out on the ranting brasses.

CROSS-COUNTRY SKIING

I love to be lured under the outstretched wings
of hemlocks heavily snowed upon, the promise
of haven they hold seductively out of the wind
beckoning me to stoop under, tilt my face
to the brashest bits that sift through. Sequestered,
I think how in the grainy videos
of refugees, snow thick as flaking plaster
falls on their razed villages. Snow
forms a cunning scrim through which the ill-clad
bent under bundles of bedding and children appear
nicely muted, trudging slow motion to provide
a generic version of misery and terror
for those who may step out of their skis to sit
under hemlock wings in all-American quiet.

THE LAST WORDS OF HENRY MANLEY

At first I thought I heard wrong. Was she sayen
Oil History Project, maybe somethen
about the year I put in ditchen, layen
roadbed up Stark Mountain in the CCC?
Liven alone, I'm shy of company
but then this girl comes prettied up in blue jeans
and has me talk into a tape machine
about my raisen. Seems it's history.

I was the raisen boy of Old Man Wasson.
Back then, the county farmed out all its orphans
to any who would have them for their keep.
My ma and pa both died in World War One.
It was the influenza took them, took down
half the town. I cried myself to sleep
one whole year, I missed my ma so terrible.
I weren't but six and scrawny. Weren't able
to do much more than clean the chicken coop

and toss hay to the goats. I weren't much good
but Old Man Wasson never used me wrong.
Because he lived alone, there were some said
he weren't right upstairs, and then they'd nod.
He fed me up on eggs and goat's milk, taught
me thirty different birds to know by song
and every plant that came. First one's coltsfoot.
Lambs' quarters is good to eat. So's cattail shoots.

Cobwebs is for cuts. Jewelweed's for the sting
of nettles. Asters bloom last. Most everythen

we ate we grew. And bartered for the rest
hayen in summer, all fall choppen wood.
Whilst I was small I stacked as best I could:
hickory, oak, maple, ash. (White birch
is only fit for tourists from the city.)
I saved my dimes for the county fair. Went dressed
up clean in Sunday clothes as if for church,
a place we never went nor never prayed.
We was a scandal to the Ladies Aid.

If there's one thing I still can't stand it's pity.
We had a handpump in the yard, a privy
a cookstove in the kitchen, a potbelly
in the front room, lamps enough to read by.
Kerosene burns yellow. I miss it still.
Not steady like a bulb, it's flickery
like somethen alive: a bird, a swallowtail.
You won't think that about 'lectricity.
And we had flowers too, old-timey ones

you hardly see these days, like hollyhocks
and red tobacco plants the hummenbirds
come to. Old Man Wasson had me listen
how those ruby throats would speak—chrk chrk—

to every bloom before they'd poke their beaks
inside. There's lots to say that don't need words.
I guess I was *his* father at the end.
He wouldn't have a doctor on the place.
I got in bed and held him till he went.

Winter of '44, private first class
in uniform like in the CCC
homesick and seasick I shipped across.
What made me famous was goen to the camps
where they'd outright starved most the men to death
and gassed the rest. Those piles of shoes and teeth?
They still come up. I dream them up in clumps.
Back home, the papers got aholt of me.
Local boy a hero in Germany.

Right here the tape clicks off. She says she's *thrilled*.
I want to say I've hardly started in
but she's packed up and standen on the doorsill
and I'm the boy whose time ran out for courten.
No one to hear me tell my other stories.
I never married. Wished I had. No roost
for this old turkey cock to share when the sun
goes down. I swung for the brass ring once, but missed
my chance. It happens. That's history.

AN INSIDER'S VIEW OF THE GARDEN

How can I help but admire the ever perseverant
unquenchable dill
that sways like an unruly crowd at a soccer match
waving its lacy banners
where garlic belongs or slyly invading a hill
of Delicata squash—
how can I help but admire such ardor? I seek it

as bees the flower's core, hummingbirds
the concocted sugar water
that lures them to the feeder in the lilacs.
I praise the springy mane
of untamed tendrils asprawl on chicken wire
that promise to bring forth
peas to overflow a pillowcase.

Some days I adore my coltish broccolis,
the sketchbook beginnings
of their green heads still encauled, incipient trees
sprung from the Pleistocene.
Some days the leeks, that Buckingham Palace patrol
and the quarter-mile of beans
—green, yellow, soy, lima, bush and pole—

demand applause. As do dilatory parsnips,
a ferny dell of tops
regal as celery. Let me laud onion that erupts
slim as a grass stem
then spends the summer inventing its pungent tulip
and the army of brussels sprouts
extending its spoon-shaped leaves over dozens of armpits

that conceal what are now merely thoughts, mere nubbins
needing long ripening.
But let me lament my root-maggot-raddled radishes
my bony and bored red peppers
that drop their lower leaves like dancehall strippers
my cauliflowers that spit
out thimblesize heads in the heat and take beetles to bed.

O children, citizens, my wayward jungly dears
you are all to be celebrated
plucked, transplanted, tilled under, resurrected here
—even the lowly despised
purslane, chickweed, burdock, poke, wild poppies.
For all of you, whether eaten or extirpated
I plan to spend the rest of my life on my knees.

ALMOST SPRING, DRIVING HOME, RECITING HOPKINS

"A devout but highly imaginative Jesuit,"
Untermeyer says in my yellowed
college omnibus of modern poets,
perhaps intending an oxymoron, but is it?
Shook foil, sharp rivers start to flow.
Landscape plotted and pieced, gray-blue, snow-pocked
begins to show its margins. Speeding back
down the interstate into my own hills
I see them *fickle, freckled*, mounded fully
and softened by millennia into pillows.
The priest's sprung metronome tick-tocks,
repeating how old winter is. It asks
each mile, snow fog battening the valleys,
what is all this juice and all this joy?

CHORES

All day he's shoveled green pine sawdust
out of the trailer truck into the chute.
From time to time he's clambered down to even
the pile. Now his hair is frosted with sawdust.
Little rivers of sawdust pour out of his boots.

I hope in the afterlife there's none of this stuff
he says, stripping nude in the late September sun
while I broom off his jeans, his sweater flocked
with granules, his immersed-in-sawdust socks.
I hope there's no bedding, no stalls, no barn

no more repairs to the paddock gate the horses
burst through when snow avalanches off the roof.
Although the old broodmare, our first foal, is his,
horses, he's fond of saying, make divorces.
Fifty years married, he's safely facetious.

No garden pump that's airbound, no window a grouse
flies into and shatters, no ancient tractor's
intractable problem with carburetor
ignition or piston, no mowers and no chain saws
that refuse to start, or start, misfire and quit.

But after a Bloody Mary on the terrace
already frost-heaved despite our heroic efforts
to level the bricks a few years back, he says
let's walk up to the field and catch the sunset
and off we go, a couple of aging fools.

I hope, he says, on the other side there's a lot
less work, but just in case I'm bringing tools.

THE WORD

We ride up softly to the hidden
oval in the woods, a plateau rimmed
with wavy stands of gray birch and white pine,
my horse thinking his thoughts, happy
in the October dapple, and I thinking
mine-and-his, which is my prerogative,

both of us just in time to see a big doe
loft up over the four-foot fence, her white scut
catching the sun and then releasing it,
soundlessly clapping our reveries shut.
The pine grove shivers as she passes.
The red squirrels thrill, announcing her departure.

Come back! I want to call to her,
we who mean you no harm. Come back and show us
who stand pinned in stopped time to the track
how you can go from a standing start
up and over. We on our side, pulses racing
are synchronized with your racing heart.

I want to tell her, Watch me
mornings when I fill the cylinders
with sunflower seeds, see how the chickadees
and lesser redbreasted nuthatches crowd
onto my arm, permitting me briefly
to stand in for a tree,

and how the vixen in the bottom meadow
I ride across allows me under cover
of horse scent to observe the education
of her kits, how they dive for the burrow
on command, how they re-emerge at another
word she uses, a word I am searching for.

Its sound is o-shaped and unencumbered,
the see-through color of river,
airy as the topmost evergreen fingers
and soft as pine duff underfoot
where the doe lies down out of sight;
take me in, tell me the word.

NEW YEAR'S EVE 1959

Remembering Anne Sexton and Jack Geiger

This was the way we used to party:
lamps unplugged, shoved in the closet
rugs rolled up, furniture pushed back
Glenn Miller singles on the spindle.

There was the poet kicking off her shoes
to jitterbug with the Physician
for Social Responsibility
the only time they ever met

and he pecking his head to the beat
swinging her out on the stalk of his arm
setting all eight gores of her skirt
twirling, then hauling her in for a Fred

Astaire session of deep dips
and both of them cutting out to strut
humming along with the riffs
that punctuated "Chattanooga Choo Choo."

This was after Seoul and before Saigon.
Coke was still a carbonated drink
we added rum to. There was French wine
but someone had misplaced the curlicue

and a not-yet famous novelist
magicked the cork out on the hinge
of the back door to "Sunrise Serenade"
and dance was the dark enabler.

Lights off a long minute at midnight
(squeals and false moans) madcap Anne
long dead now and Jack snowily
balding who led the drive to halt the bomb
and I alone am saved to tell you
how they could jive.

OCTOBER, YELLOWSTONE PARK

How happy the animals seem just now,
all reading the sweetgrass text, heads down
in the great yellow-green sea of the high plains—
antelope, bison, the bull elk and his cows

moving commingled in little clumps, the bull
elk bugling from time to time his rusty screech
but not yet in rut, the females not yet in heat,
peacefully inattentive—the late fall

asters still blooming, the glacial creeks running clear.
What awaits them this winter—which calves will starve
to death or driven by hunger stray from the park
to be shot on the cattle range—they are unaware.

It is said that dumb beasts cannot anticipate
though for terror of fire or wolves some deep
historical memory clangs out of sleep
pricking them to take flight. As flight pricked the poet

dead seventeen years today, who for seventeen
years before that was a better sister
than any I, who had none, could have conjured.
Dead by her own hand, who so doggedly whined

at Daddy Death's elbow that the old Squatter
at last relented and took her in. Of sane mind
and body aged but whole I stand by the sign
that says we are halfway between the equator

and the North Pole. Sad but celebratory
I stand in full sun on the 45th parallel
bemused by what's to come, by what befell,
by how our friendship flared into history.

Fair warning, Annie, there will be no more
elegies, no more direct-address songs
conferring the tang of loss, its bitter flavor
as palpable as alum on the tongue.

Climbing up switchbacks all this afternoon,
sending loose shale clattering below,
grimly, gradually ascending to a view
of snowcaps and geysers, the balloon

of Old Faithful spewing, I hear your voice
beside me (you, who hated so to sweat!)
cheerfully cursing at eight thousand feet
the killers of the dream, the small-time advice-

laden editors and hangers-on. I've come
this whole hard way alone to an upthrust slate
above a brace of eagles launched in flight
only to teeter, my equilibrium

undone by memory. I want to fling
your cigarette- and whiskey-hoarse chuckle
that hangs on inside me down the back wall
over Biscuit Basin. I want the painting

below to take me in. My world that threatened
to stop the day you stopped, faltered
and then resumed, unutterably altered.
Where wildfires crisped its hide and blackened

whole vistas, new life inched in. My map
blooms with low growth, sturdier than before.
Thus I abstain. I will not sing, except
of the elk and his harem who lie down in grandeur

on the church lawn at Mammoth Hot Springs,
his hat rack wreathed in mist. This year's offspring
graze in the town's backyards, to the dismay
of tenants who burst out to broom them away.

May the car doors of tourists slam, may cameras go wild
staying the scene, may the occasional
antelope slip into the herd, shy as a child.
May people be ravished by this processional.

May reverence for what lopes off to the hills
at dusk be imprinted on their brain pans
forever, as on mine. As you are, Anne.
All of you hammered golden against the anvil.

AFTER THE POETRY READING

for Marie Howe

If Emily Dickinson lived in the 2000s
and let herself have sex appeal
she'd grow her hair wild and electric
down to her buttocks, you said. She'd wear
magenta tights, black ankle socks
and tiny pointed paddock boots.

Intrigued, I saw how Emily'd
master Microsoft, how she'd
fax the versicles that Higginson
advised her not to print to MS.
APR and Thirteenth Moon.

She'd read aloud at benefits
address the weavers' guild
the garden club, the anarchists
Catholics for free choice
welfare moms, the Wouldbegoods
and the Temple Sinai sisterhood.

Thinking the same thing, silent
we see Emily flamboyant.
Her words for the century to come
are pithy, oxymoronic.
Her fly buzzes me all the way home.

GUS SPEAKS

I was the last of my line,
farm-raised, chesty, and bold.
Not one of your flawless show-world
forty-five-pound Dalmatians.
I ran with the horses, my darlings.

I loped at their heels, mile
for mile, swam rivers they forded
wet to the belly. I guarded
them grazing, haloed in flies.
Their smell became my smell.

Joyous I ate their manure.
Its undigested oats
still sweet, kept me fit.
I slept curled at the flank
of the fiercest broodmare.

We lay, a study in snores
ear flicks and farts in her stall
until she came to the brink,
the birth hour of her foal.
Then, she shunned me cruelly.

Spring and fall I erred over
and over. Skunks were my folly.
Then, I was nobody's lover.
I rolled in dung and sand.
When my heart burst in the pond,

my body sank and then rose
like a birch log, a blaze
of white against spring green.
Now I lie under the grasses
they crop, my own swift horses

who start up and spook in the rain
without me, the warm summer rain.

FROM THE 18TH FLOOR

for Hilma Wolitzer

Sunrise is a peach curtain,
the river a woman
in a lamé dress. Noon, its
slats up, a wide heaven,
dusk a soundless
opera, orange-tinged.

Down there, people reduce
to insects, the dry pods
of their commonplace
griefs, desires, occasional
joys tiny ramrods
within the scuttle that propels
them so grace-
fully backwards and forwards.

We who are merely
the guests of insects,
twelve times outweighed
by them on this planet,
breathe lightly at the window.
We admire the clean
confusion below
such as God might have seen
circling at this height,
deciding not to land

so that when
the knife-scream of rescue wagons
comes faintly through glass
it is less a sound than
a shape, a passing caress
up here where we impend
keeping an aesthetic distance,
large old friends.

BEANS BEANS BEANS

for Yann

My grandson and I are doing up the beans
together to be blanched, then frozen.
We are singing *beans beans beans*
they make you feel so mean
on the farm on the farm.
Last week he shaved his head at soccer camp
—immediate regret—already it
is fuzzing over with biracial curls.

The green beans are Provider, bush. The yellow,
Kentucky Wonder, pole. The way I sort
is for convenience: size, not species.
They make a lovely mix, as do Yann's genes.
I like to think someday the world will be
one color, more or less. The word
is heterosis, hybrid vigor,
from the Greek for alteration.

Consider these beans, meanwhile, Provider
podding early, each plant a sturdy city,
roots like subways fanning out. The later
Wonders wrap creatively around
whatever's been set out for them:
poplar saplings, wire, twine,
winding, crosshatching, hanging on,
tying knots like boyish sailors
scrambling up the rigging toward the sun.

Take this crop in aggregate
shading from churned butter with flecks
of palest green to forest green, and take
this boy who helps to top and tail
a basketful with me, a creature leaping
between bush and pole.

THE RIDDLE OF NOAH

You want to change your name. You're looking
for "something more suitable," words we can only guess
you've come by from television or teachers. All
your first-grade friends have names like Justin Mark
Caroline Emma or newly enrolled Xuan Loc
and yours, you sadly report, is Noah . . . nothing.

Noah *Hodges*, your middle name isn't nothing
your mother, named Hodges, reproves, but you go on looking.
Next day you are somebody else: Adam Stinger! The clock
turns back to my brother, Edward Elias, whose quest
to be named for his father (living names are death marks
on a Jewish child) was fulfilled by a City Hall

clerk. Peter Jr. went gladly to school all
unblessed. The names that we go by are nothing
compared to the names we are called. *Christ killer!* they mocked
and stoned me with quinces in my bland-looking
suburb. Why didn't I tattle, resist? I guessed
I was guilty, the only kid on my manicured block

who didn't know how to genuflect as we lock-
stepped to chapel at noontime. I was in thrall,
the one Jewish girl in my class at Holy Ghost
convent school. Xuan Loc, which translates as something
magical and tender—Spring Bud, a way of looking
at innocence—is awarded the gold bookmark

for reading more chapter-books than Justin Mark
or Noah, who now has tears in his eyes. No lack
of feeling here, a jealous Yahweh is looking
over his shoulder hissing, Be best of all.
What can be done to ease him? Nothing
makes up for losing, though love is a welcome guest.

Spared being burned at the stake, being starved or gassed,
like Xuan Loc, Noah is fated to make his mark,
suffer for grace through good works, aspire to something.
Half-Jewish, half-Christian, he will own his name, will unlock
the riddle of who he is: only child, in equal
measure blessed and damned to be inward-looking,

always slightly aslant the mark, like Xuan Loc.
Always playing for keeps, for all or nothing
in quest of his rightful self while the world looks on.

CONNECTING THE DOTS

I think Daddy
just dropped dead
(our son at five)
I'll drive the car
and now they drive
us living, the large

children home
a week at Christmas
ten days in August
posing for
the family snapshot
flanked by dogs.

We're assayed kindly
to see if we're
still competent
to keep house, mind
the calendar
connect the dots.

Well, we're still stack-
ing wood for winter
turning compost
climbing ladders
and they still love us
who overtake us

who want what's best
for us, who sound
(deep reservoirs
of patience) the way
we did, or like
to think we did.

THE LONG MARRIAGE

SKINNYDIPPING WITH WILLIAM WORDSWORTH

I lie by the pond *in utter nakedness*
thinking of you, Will, your epiphanies
of woodcock, raven, rills, and craggy steeps,
the solace that seductive nature bore,
and how in my late teens I came to you
with other Radcliffe *pagans suckled in*
a creed outworn, declaiming whole swatches
of "Intimations" to each other.

Moist-eyed with reverence, lying about
the common room, rising to recite
Great God! I'd rather be . . . How else
redeem the first flush of experience?
How else create it again and again? *Not in*
entire forgetfulness I raise up my boyfriend,
a Harvard man who could outquote me
in his Groton elocutionary style.

Groping to unhook my bra he swore
poetry could change the world for the better.
The War was on. Was I to let him die
unfulfilled? Soon afterward we parted.
Years later, he a decorated vet,
I a part-time professor, signed the same
guest book in the Lake District. Stunned
by coincidence we gingerly shared a room.

Ah, Will, high summer now; how many more
of these? *Fair seed-time had my soul,*
you sang; what seed-times still to come?
How I mistrust them, cheaters that will flame,
gutter and go out, like the scarlet tanager
who lights in the apple tree but will not stay.

Here at the pond, your *meadow, grove, and stream*
lodged in my head as tight as lily buds,
sun slants through translucent minnows, dragonflies
in paintbox colors couple in midair.
The fickle tanager flies over the tasseled field.
I lay my "Prelude" down under the willow.
My old gnarled body prepares to swim
to the other side.
                    Come with me, Will.
Let us cross over sleek as otters,
each of us bobbing in the old-fashioned breaststroke,
each of us centered in our beloved Vales.

THINKING OF GORKI WHILE CLEARING A TRAIL

It wasn't exactly raining but
a little wetness still dribbled down.
I had been reading and sorrowing
and set out with the dogs as an antidote.
They went ahead snuffling in the leaf plaster.
Despite the steady snick of my clippers
boletus mushrooms kept popping soundlessly
out of the ground. How else account for
the ones with mouse-bites out of the caps
when I doubled back on my tracks?

The animals have different enzymes
from us. They can eat amanitas
we die of. The woodpeckers' fledglings
clack like a rattle of drumsticks each time
crumpled dragonflies arrive and are thrust
into the bud vases of their gullets.
The chipmunk crosses in front of me
tail held up like a banner. Who knows
what he has in his cheeks? Beechnuts
would be good, or a morsel of amanita.

Gorki disliked his face with its high
Mongol cheekbones. *It would be good to be
a bandit*, he said, *to rob rich misers
and give their money to the poor.* Saturnine
Gorki, at the 1929 International Congress
of Atheists. By then he was famous, but
twice, in his teens, he tried to kill
himself. Called before an ecclesiastical
tribunal and excommunicated, he declared
God is the name of my desire.

The animals have no Holy Synod to
answer to. They simply pursue their vocations.
In general, I desire to see God lifting
the needy up out of their dung heap,
as it is written. I did not seek this
ancient porcupine curled in the hollow
of a dead ash tree, delicately encoded
on top of a mountain of his own dung,
pale buff-colored pellets that must have
taken several seasons to accumulate.

At this moment, I desire the dogs, oblivious
so far, not to catch sight or scent of him.
I am the rightful master of my soul
Gorki said, and is this not true of the porcupine?
Born Aleksei Maksimovich Peshkov
he chose his own name—*gorki*—bitter
and a century later I carry him
like a pocket guide on this secret trail
clearing and wool-gathering as we go.

IMAGINING MARIANNE MOORE
IN THE BUTTERFLY GARDEN

Surrounded, blundered into by
these gorgeous tropical ephemerae,
we watch their pinwheel colors compose
an arcane calligraphy on air
under a quarter-acre of fine mesh.

I almost step on a slender young botanist
in a shocking-pink smock, lying flat
to pollinate certain recalcitrant flowers
with a single-haired paintbrush.
You bend to inspect her handiwork
your twice-wound braids frizzing red against
the sun to form a sort of web.

Marianne, I was appalled you dared
to chloroform a cat and then
dissect it at Bryn Mawr. Was it
the miniaturist impulse even then,
a schoolgirl's red desire
to see fine things in place?

When our guide uses her second and third
fingers to clasp a palm-size Heliconid
by one wing, you murmur approvingly,
Precisionist. We peer at the owl eye it wears
as a scare tactic. I see a frisson pierce you
just as the peacocks on the grass at Oxford
once made your hair stand on end, the eyes
of their tail feathers holding you fast.

Worlds apart we are undergraduates
again. Letting the brilliant mimicry
shiver through us.
We are the beasts, you whisper
and I nod, releasing you.
The noiseless Heliconid
soars to another silent flower.

PANTOUM, WITH SWAN

for Carolyn Kizer

Bits of his down under my fingernails
a gob of his spit behind one ear
and a nasty welt where the nib of his beak
bit down as he came. It was our first date.

A gob of his spit behind one ear,
his wings still fanning. I should have known better,
I should have bitten him off on our first date.
And yet for some reason I didn't press charges;

I wiped off the wet. I should have known better.
They gave me the morning-after pill
and shook their heads when I wouldn't press charges.
The yolk that was meant to hatch as Helen

failed to congeal, thanks to the morning-after pill
and dropped harmlessly into the toilet
so that nothing became of the lost yolk, Helen,
Troy, wooden horse, forestalled in one swallow

flushed harmlessly away down the toilet.
The swan had by then stuffed Euripedes, Sophocles
—leaving out Helen, Troy, Agamemnon—
the whole house of Atreus, the rest of Greek tragedy,

stuffed in my head, every strophe of Sophocles.
His knowledge forced on me, yet Bird kept the power.
What was I to do with ancient Greek history
lodged in my cortex to no avail?

I had his knowledge, I had no power
the year I taught Yeats in a classroom so pale
that a mist enshrouded the ancient religions
and bits of his down flew from under my fingernails.

THE BROWN MOUNTAIN

What dies out of us and our creatures,
out of our fields and gardens,
comes slowly back to improve us:
the entire mat of nasturtiums
after frost has blackened them,
sunflower heads the birds
have picked clean, the still
sticky stalks of milkweed
torn from the pasture, coffee grounds,
eggshells, moldy potatoes,
the tough little trees that once
were crowded with brussels sprouts,
tomatoes cat-faced or bitten into
by inquisitive chipmunks,
gargantuan cucumbers gone soft
from repose. Not the corn stalks and shucks,
not windfall apples. These
are sanctified by the horses.
The lettuces are revised
as rabbit pellets, holy with nitrogen.
Whatever fodder is offered the sheep
comes back to us as raisins
of useful dung.

Compost is our future.
The turgid brown mountain
steams, releasing
the devil's own methane vapor,
cooking our castoffs so that from
our spatterings and embarrassments—
cat vomit, macerated mice,
rotten squash, burst berries,
a mare's placenta, failed melons,
dog hair, hoof parings—arises
a rapture of blackest humus.
Dirt to top-dress, dig in. Dirt fit
for the gardens of commoner and king.

HIGHWAY HYPOTHESIS

Nothing quite rests the roving eye
like this long view of sloping fields
that rise to a toyshop farmhouse
with matchstick barns and sheds.
A large yellow beetle spits silage
onto an upturned cricket while
several inch-high cars and trucks
flow soundlessly up the spitcurl drive.

Bucophilia, I call it—
nostalgia over a pastoral vista—
where for all I know the farmer
who owns it or rents it just told his
wife he'd kill her if she left him and
she did and he did and now here come
the auctioneer, the serious bidders
and an ant-train of gawking onlookers.

GHAZAL: ON THE TABLE

I was taught to smooth the aura at the end,
said my masseuse, hands hovering at the end.

Inches above my placid pummeled self
did I feel something floating at the end?

Or is my naked body merely prone
to ectoplasmic vapors to no end?

Many other arthritics have lain here
seeking to roll pain's boulder end on end.

Herbal oils, a CD playing soft
loon calls, wave laps, bird trills now must end.

I rise and dress, restored to lift and bend,
my ethereal wisp invisible at the end.

GRADY, WHO LOST A LEG IN KOREA, ADDRESSES ME IN THE REHAB GYM

He fondles the stump.
See these here flaps along the seam?
Dog ears, they're called.
Gotta work em down
like pie dough with a roller pin
get em smooth enough to set against
the fiberglass. It's light as eggshell.
Gwan, try my leg. Pick it up.

Never could wear the one
they fit me to at the V.A.
Mostly metal, weighed a ton
to cart around, but now—
nodding at another amputee
practicing between
the parallel bars—*I'm gonna*
give it another try.

Grady calls me Parrot Head
—the metal cage that holds
my broken neck—I call him Ahab.
Even though we're little more
than fellow inmates in
the neuro unit on the topmost floor
down here we're life companions
makin a game of it.

Now those guys over there
in chairs? They got the sugar.
Diabetes. Works like a cannibal,
one leg, then the other.
Toes first, foot next, then the knee.
And when they got no other way
to stop the rot, they saw
the goddamn leg off up to here.

He draws his hand across his groin.
Can't fit a thing to that.
You gotta have a stump.
They call em double amputees.
You see em outside on good days
doin wheelies, rearin back
to jump the sidewalk curb
like a bunch of acrobats

makin a game of it.
And once I get the hang of this
I'm gonna waltz my way around
the gym. And then
I'm gonna ask you, Parrot Head,
Wanna dance?

IDENTIFYING THE DISAPPEARED

The exiles have returned from safe cold places
with their resistance to forgetting, returned
with brush and spoon, sieve and dustpan
to bring back the bones of a child, which are become
the bones of a nesting bird; the lip of a clavicle
transformed into angel wings which want to be
its mother; skulls for uncle, father, brother
who soiled themselves and died in the Resistance.

It is another day to walk about
testing the earth for springy places to insert
their tools, another day to see what the dead
saw in that instant after the machete
severed the critical artery,
after the eye went milky and the soul
flew away in horror and the flesh retreated
in narrow strips, like ribbons, from the bone.

The exiles have come back. They are breaking
the sleep of earth, they are packing the dry shards
of the disappeared in cardboard cartons
Relief provides—wood is scarce here—
and still they store up the names of the murderers
who have put away their uniforms and persuasions
under the landmine of respectability,
the trigger, God willing, one day they will trip on.

BRINGING DOWN THE BIRDS

for Christopher Cokinos

Does it make you wince to hear
how the last of the world's great auks
were scalded to death on the Newfoundland coast
in vats of boiling water so that
birdshot would not mutilate the feathers
that stuffed the mattress your great-grandparents
lay upon, begetting your forebears?

Are you uncomfortable reading how
the flocks of passenger pigeons
that closed over the sky like an eyelid
the millions that roared like thunder
like trains, like tornados were wiped out, expunged
in a free-for-all a hundred years gone?
Can you bear the metaphor in how it was done?

Pet pigeons, their eyelids sewn, were tied
to stools a few feet off the ground until
hordes of their kind swooped overhead.
Released, their downward flutter lured
the multitude who were smothered in nets
while trappers leaped among them
snapping their necks with pincers.
The feathers from fifty pigeons
added up to a pound of bedding.

Does it help to name the one-or-two-of-a-kind
Martha or Rollie and exhibit them in a zoo
a kindly zoo with moats in place of wire
or clone from fished-up bits of DNA
a creature rather like the creature
it had been, left to the whim of nature?

Would bringing the ivorybill back from deep woods
to a greenhouse earth placate the gods?
The harlequin-patterned Labrador duck
the dowdy heath hen, the gregarious Carolina parakeet
that once bloomed like daffodils in flight,
if science could reconstruct them, how long
would it take us logging and drilling and storing up
treasures to do them all in again?

WANT

The world is awash in unwanted dogs:
look-alike yellow curly-tailed mongrels that come
collared and wormed, neutered and named, through customs
come immunized, racketing and rabies-tagged

to Midwestern farms from Save the Children, the Peace Corps
come from Oxfam into the carpeted bedrooms of embassies
into the Brooklyn lofts of CARE workers on leave
the London, Paris, Geneva homes of Doctors Without Borders

and still the streets of Asmara, Kigali, Bombay
refill with ur-dogs: those bred-back scavenging flea-ridden
sprung-ribbed bitches whose empty teats make known
the latest bitten-off litter of curs that go back to the Pleistocene.

And what of the big-headed stick-figured children naked
in the doorways of Goma, Luanda, Juba, Les Hants
or crouched in the dust of haphazard donkey-width tracks
that connect the named and the nameless hamlets of Want?

There will always be those who speed past unbeguiled.
There will always be somewhere a quorum of holy fools
who wade into the roiling sea despite the tsunami
to dip teaspoon after teaspoon from the ocean.

THE LONG MARRIAGE

The sweet jazz
of their college days
spools over them
where they lie
on the dark lake
of night growing
old unevenly:
the sexual thrill
of Pee Wee Russell's
clarinet; Jack
Teagarden's trombone
half syrup, half
sobbing slide;
Erroll Garner's
rusty hum-along
over the ivories;
and Glenn Miller's
plane going down
again before sleep
repossesses them. . . .

Torschlusspanik.
Of course
the Germans have
a word for it,
the shutting of
the door,
the bowels' terror
that one will go
before
the other as
the clattering horse
hooves near.

JOHN GREEN TAKES HIS WARNER, NEW HAMPSHIRE, NEIGHBOR TO A RED SOX GAME

Everett down the hill's
52 and trim. No beer gut.
Raises beef, corn, hay, cuts
cordwood between harvests.
Goes to bed at 8 and falls
into sleep like a parachutist.

He's never been to a ballgame.
He's never been to Boston though
he went over to Portland, Maine
one time ten, fifteen years ago.

In Sullivan Square, they
luck out, find a space
for John's car, take
the T to Fenway Park.
The famous T!
A kind of underground trolley.
Runs in the dark.
No motorman that Ev can see.
Jammed with other sports fans.

John has to show him
how to put the token in.
How to press with his hips
to go through the turnstile.
How to stand back while
the doors whoosh shut.
How to grab a strap
as the car pitches forward.
How to push out
with the surging crowd.

Afterward Ev says the game's
a whole lot better on TV.
Too many fans.
Too many other folks for him.

FLYING

When Mother was little, all
that she knew about flying was what
her bearded grandfather told her:
every night your soul flies
out of your body and into
God's lap. He keeps it under
his handkerchief until morning.

Hearing this as a child haunted me.
I couldn't help sleeping.
I woke up each morning groping
as for a lost object lodged perhaps
between my legs, never knowing
what had been taken from me or what
had been returned to its harbor.

When as a new grandmother
my mother first flew cross-country
—the name of the airline escapes me
but the year was 1947—
she consigned her soul to the Coco-
Chanel-costumed stewardess
then ordered a straight-up martini.

As they landed, the nose wheel wobbled
and dropped away. Some people screamed.
My mother was not one of them
but her shoes—she had slipped them off—
somersaulted forward. Deplaning
she took out her handkerchief
and reclaimed her soul from the ashen stewardess.

That night in a room not her own
under eaves heavy with rain
and the rue of a disbelieving daughter
my mother described her grandfather to me
a passionate man who carried his soul
wedged deep in his pants' watch-pocket:
a pious man whose red beard had never seen scissors

who planted his carrots and beets
in the dark of the moon for good reason
and who, before I was born,
rose up like Elijah.
Flew straightaway up into heaven.

GIVING BIRTH

for Yann, at nineteen

Every month I went to the obstetrician. The sign
over his examining table said: Familiarity
Breeds. Every month I lay down on the hard slab
to be poked and peered at, or—this was before ultrasound—
palpated per rectum. Every month I answered
the same perfunctory questions:
Any trouble with our waterworks? Are we sleeping?
Every month I was ushered out by Dr. Congeniality
as if this were indeed a joint enterprise
and not the singular journey I took three times.

No father was permitted to attend.
No mother to be conscious during the crossing.
Painkillers and truth serums were the drugs of choice.
I thrashed and swore furiously, I was told, ex post facto.
My vocabulary astonished the interns.
Thus Demeroled and scopolamined, my body
slammed through the waves without me
only taking me back in when a face
leaned over mine each time in the recovery room
and said, Congratulations. You have a girl.
You have a girl. You have a boy.

Even after landfall I was held in bed.
During the week-long stay in Maternity no infant
could cross the threshold of the four-mothers-to-a-room
except at feeding time. The medley
of sobbing babies being trundled up and down
the corridor at 6-10-2-6-10
swelled and subsided, tragic doppler music

so that when your mother nineteen years ago
asked me to be her birth partner, I swelled
with prestige. I went to birthing classes
for the breathing, the panting, the back rubs.
I packed special teas and lotions.
Ever efficient, she went into labor before my plane
had touched down on the far side of the Atlantic.

Darkness drifted on us from the mountains.
We drove to the hospital pausing between contractions.
The midwives—one spoke German,
the other, French—installed us in a bedroom
wallpapered with nosegays of roses.
No metal crib sides. No stirrups. Everyone
was eerily cheerful. The boyish doctor
strode in still clutching his motorcycle helmet
seemingly uneasy in this gathering of women,
content to be a bit player unless needed.

Painfully and with enormous effort your mother opened.
Mottled purple and black-haired, an unexpected
animal emerged from the tunnel. I gasped.
The midwives handed me this hard foreign muscle
that flexed and contracted from the shock of entry.
I held it in a shallow basin of warm water
and sloshed it with antiseptic soap to remove
the coating it had come with and then carried it
to the bed where it magicked into the baby
your mother had brought forth and now put to her breast.

You slept in the curl of your mother's body
as we four women drank champagne
and ate zwieback and congratulated each other.
At first light, driving your mother's little Renault
I followed the German-speaking midwife
back through the unfamiliar streets
back to the converted farmhouse overlooking
the border crossing where we honked farewells
and the sun came up unsurprised.

THE COLLECTION

In Gestapo-ridden Paris, Bertrand,
a boy I met once he was safe in Queens,
cruised the Métro nightly with a razor
blade concealed between his fingers
for harvesting sundry decorations
from the chests of sodden German soldiers.

Only child, too young to be a courier
in the Resistance, he spent the year he should
have been bar mitzvahed slept against,
felt up, and vomited on. He loved geometry
even then, at home in three dimensions,
grew up to be an astrophysicist.

No drama in the rest of Bertrand's life
spent measuring black holes, red giants,
could match the terror in the slither
of his fingers, the thrill of slicing
trophies from their moorings, then pocketing
the stash to add to his collection.

He brought it to the States in bonbon boxes,
one for ribbons and tinny iron crosses,
the other for thickly tarnished buttons,
and kept them in a knapsack under his bed.
High school seniors, we clung to each other
while his parents divorced, that year in Queens

but when I spent the night in Bertrand's bed
he unpacked and fondled his treasures
as if I were no longer there.

THREE DREAMS AFTER A SUICIDE

—Anne Sexton, 1974

1.

We're gathered in the funeral home, your friends
who are not themselves especially friends,
with you laid out on view in the approved fashion
wearing the bright-red reading dress with cut-glass buttons
that wink at the ceiling, when you spring
like a jack-in-the-box from the coffin
crying Boo! I was only fooling!

2.

After the terrible whipping you are
oddly pleased with yourself,
an impenitent child, the winner.
It's Daddy Death who's quit.
Once more you've worn him out
from all his lifting and striking.
His belt lies shredded in his meaty fist.

3.

We are standing together in a sunless garden
in Rockport, Mass. I'm wearing the hat
the artist painted you in
and suddenly swarms of wasps
fly up under the downturned brim.

O death, where is thy sting?
Tar baby, it is stickered to me; you
were my wasp and I your jew.

OBLIVION

The dozen ways they did it—
off a bridge, the back of a boat,
pills, head in the oven, or
wrapped in her mother's old mink coat
in the garage, a brick on the accelerator,
the Cougar's motor thrumming
while she crossed over.

What they left behind—
the outline of a stalled novel, diaries,
their best poems, the note that ends
now will you believe me,
offspring of various ages, spouses
who cared and weep and yet
admit relief now that it's over.

How they fester, the old details
held to the light like a stained-glass icon
—the shotgun in the mouth, the string
from toe to trigger; the tongue
a blue plum forced between his lips
when he hanged himself in her closet—
for us it is never over

who raced to the scene, cut the noose,
pulled the bathtub plug on pink water,
broke windows, turned off the gas,
rode in the ambulance, only minutes later
to take the body blow of bad news.
We are trapped in the plot, every one.
Left behind, there is no oblivion.

JACK AND OTHER NEW POEMS

NEW HAMPSHIRE, FEBRUARY 7, 2003

It's snowing again.
All day, reruns
of the blizzard of '78
newscasters vying
for bragging rights
how it was to go hungry
after they'd thumped
the vending machines empty
the weatherman clomping
four miles on snowshoes
to get to his mike
so he could explain
how three lows
could collide to create
a lineup of isobars
footage of state troopers
peering into the caked
windows of cars
backed up for white
miles on the interstate.

No reruns today
of the bombings in Vietnam
2 million civilians blown
apart, most of them children
under 16, children
always the least

able to dive
for cover when
all that tonnage bursts
from a blind sky.
Snow here is
weighting the pine trees
while we wait for the worst:
for war to begin.
Schools closed, how
the children
love a benign blizzard
a downhill scrimmage
of tubes and sleds. But who
remembers the blizzard
that burst on those other children?
Back then we called it
collateral damage
and will again.

FOX ON HIS BACK

homage to Theodore Roethke

On long nights shy of melt
implacable and clear
wind drilling the last leaf
the poet to play it safe
slept with a baby's quilt
pulled over his bald head.
O what's the winter for?
To remember love, he said.

Fox on his back in a hole
snake eyes in the wall asleep
grubs shellacked in their coils
sap locked tight to the pith
roots sucking a hollow tooth
a brown and pregnant bear
leaf-wrapped like an old cigar. . . .

O what's the winter for?
the quilted poet asked.
Doors slam overhead
as maple buffets ash.
To remember love, he said.

WIDOW AND DOG

After he died she started letting the dog
sleep on his side of the bed they had shared
for fifty-one years. A large discreet dog, he stayed
on his side but the tags on his collar jingled as he sighed
and especially when he scratched so she took his collar off
and then his smooth tawny bulk close to her but not
touching eased her through the next night and the next.

One morning, a chipmunk and his wife somehow slipped in
through the screen door when neither of them was looking.
She got up screaming from her coffee and whacked at them
with a broom. Dog pounced and pounced but they were faster
than he was and dove under the refrigerator. After a while
he stopped crashing into chairs and skidding around corners
in fruitless pursuit and then they came and went untroubled
even drinking out of his water dish, their tails at right angles.

That summer it just seemed simpler to leave the window
by the bird feeder open for ease of refilling. Some creatures
slipped casually out and in. The titmice were especially graceful.
She loved to watch them elevate and retract their crests
whenever they perched on the lips of the kitchen counters.
The goldfinches chittered and sang like drunken canaries
and once in a thunderstorm a barred owl blundered
into that fake crystal chandelier she had always detested.

Autumn fell on them in a joyous rush. The first
needles of hard frost, the newly sharp wind, the final
sweep and swirl of leaves, a swash of all-day rain
were not unwelcome. Hickory nuts ricocheted
off the barn's metal roof like a rain of beebee-gun pellets.
They both took afternoon naps. They both grew portly.
While Dog in his dumb allegiance dozed on the hearth,
sometimes he ran so fiercely in his dreams that he bared his teeth.
Reclusive comfortable Widow scribbled in her journal.
It did not matter how much she woolgathered, how late
into the night she read, it did not matter if she
completed this poem, or another.

THE SUNDAY PHONE CALL

Drab December, sleet falling.
Dogs loosely fisted in torpor.
Horses nose-down in hay.
It's the hour, years ago
I used to call my parents
or they'd call me.

The phone rings. Idly
empty of expectation
I answer. It's my father's
voice. *Pop!* I say, *you're dead!*
Don't you remember
that final heart attack
Dallas, just before
Kennedy was shot?

Time means nothing here,
kiddo. He's jolly, expansive.
You can wait eons for an open line.
Time gets used up but
comes back, you know.
Like Ping-Pong.

Ping-Pong! The table in
the attic. My father, shirtsleeves
rolled, the wet stub of
a burnt-out cigarette
stuck to his lower lip as
he murdered each one
of my three older brothers
and me yearning under the eaves
waiting for my turn.

You sound . . . just like yourself
I say. *I am myself, goddammit!*
Anyway, what's this
about an accident?

How did you hear about it?

I read it somewhere. Broke
your neck, etcetera.
He says this vaguely
his shorthand way
of keeping feelings at bay.

You mean you read
my memoir? Did
you know you're in it?

Didn't read that part. No
reason to stir things up.
Now I'm indignant.
But I almost died!

Didn't I tell you
never buy land on a hill?
It's worthless. What's
an educated dame like you
doing messing with horses?
Messing with horses is
for punks. (Then, a little
softer), *I see you two've*
put a lot of work into
that hunk of real estate.

Thanks. Thanks for even
noticing. We love it here.
We'll never sell.

Like hell you won't!
You will!

Pop, I say, tearing up,
let's not fight for once.
My only Poppa, when
do I get to see you?
A long pause. Then
coughing his cigarette cough
Pupchen, he says
I may be dead but
I'm not clairvoyant.
Behave yourself.
The line clicks off.

MAGDA OF HOSPICE HOUSE

They call me Maggie here.
I love my work as specialist in easement.

Now I am naturalized and marketable.
Death is the thing I know, its catch and gurgle.

I oversee the art of dying—art
is what we try to make of it

with music and good wines,
old-fashioned beds as deep as cradles,

down pillows, percale sheets. And isn't it odd?
Juicy Fruit gum. I like to think

our ministrations, the bent straw slaking
morphine thirst, can alter history a little.

*I am so sad I have come out
on the other side*, the poet wrote

before he died, but all of us
one day will cross that boundary.

I crossed the Danube first on an inner tube
the summer of '89. My name was Magda then.

I was too full of empty deaths
to stay, too full of machine-gunnings,

hangings, orphans unfed to the end,
bloodbaths in ancient Timisoara,

and then the tyrant's orders to shoot
into the swollen crowds in Bucharest. . . .

Nixon gave Ceauşescu a Buick limousine!
I crossed to take my chances in

Yugoslavia—it was still Yugoslavia
back then—and gladly served six weeks' detention.

When Nikolai and Elena, hands bound, went down
before the firing squad I exulted.

Although I am faithless, I ♥ my new New York.
I can recite the "Stabat Mater," also Kaddish.

I love rocking my great bony babies
away in my arms, Demerol tucked in their cheeks,

or easing them onto the stallions' withers
and clapping them off for that final gallop

over the desert. O may we all come out
as softly dead as they on the other side.

SEVEN CAVEATS IN MAY

When the dog whines at 5 a.m., do not
make your first mistake and let him out.
When he starts to bark in a furious tom-tom rhythm
and you can just discern a shadowy feinting

taking place under the distant hemlocks
do not seize the small sledge from the worktable and fly
out there in your nightgown and unlaced high
tops preparing to whack this, the ninth of its kind

in the last ten weeks, over the head
before it can quill your canine.
But it's not a porcupine: it's a big, black, angry
bear. Now your dog has put him up a tree

and plans to keep him there, a perfect
piece of work by any hound. Do not
run back and grab the manure fork
thinking you can keep the prongs

between you and the elevated bear long
enough to dart in and corral your critter.
Isn't it true bears come down slower
than they go up? Half an hour later do not

give up, go in the house and call the cops.
The dispatcher regrets having to report
there's no patrol car at this time, the state
police are covering. No doubt the nearest

trooper, wearing his Smokey Bear Stetson
is forty miles up the highway.
When your closest neighbor, big burly Smitty
works his way into his jeans and roars up

your dirt road in his four-wheel diesel truck
strides over the slash pile and hauls your hound back
(by now, you've thrown something on
over your not-quite-diaphanous nightgown)

do not forget to thank him with a six-pack.
Do not fail to take your feeders in on April One
despite the arriving birds' insistent clamor
and do not put them out again

until the first of December.

SUMMER MEDITATION

It isn't gunfire
that wakes me
but the rat-a-tat-tat
of hickory nuts raining
on the tin roof
of the trailer barn.
Then the barred owl
in the blackness, calling
for company, who
who cooks for you-u-u?
and suddenly
it's morning.

In the bathroom
the tiny phallic
night light
still flickers.
Black spots
of gnats, moths
folded in slumber
with one swipe
of the washcloth
reduce to powder.
An earwig to flush.
Two mosquitoes
lurking in the shower.
Killing before
breakfast

and killing after:
Japanese beetles
all green and coppery
fornicating on
the leafy tops
of the raspberries
piggybacked
triplets and foursomes
easy to flick
into soap suds.
Their glistening
drowning selves
a carpet of beads unstrung
spit Bad Buddhist!

At the pond
naked, pale
I slip between
two shores
of greenery
solitary
back in the murk
of womb while
there goes mr. big
the brookie
trailed by mrs. big
wispy silhouettes

darting in synchrony
past the deep pool
by the great rock

the great rock
that is always dark
on its underside
the one I used to dive
from, aiming to come up
in the heart
of a cold spring
rising exultant
time after time
into the fizz
of lime-green light. . . .

At sundown the horses'
winter hay arrives.
The dogs raise
an appropriate racket.
Always the annual
hay supply comes
at suppertime
on the hottest day
of August.

Eddy and Tim, oily
with sweat, grunt
bucking hay
heaving
40-lb. bales up
crisscrossed like
Pick-Up Sticks
so air can circulate.
They stand around after
holding their elbows
that noncommittal
Yankee gesture
that says friendship
same as last year.
We chat, exchange
town gossip
the usual, except
Eddie's son
is in Iraq.

Afterward
the sweep-up.
Hay clings to everything
like rumor.
The full barn
cries summer, a scent
I suck into myself.

Big red sundown
induces melancholy.

I want to sing
of death unbruised.
Its smoothening.
I want to prepare
for death's arrival
in my life.
I want to be
an advanced thinker—
the will, the organ donation,
the power of attorney—
but when my old
dead horses come
running toward me
in a dream
healthy and halterless
—Gennie, Taboo, and Jack—
I take it back.

If only death could be
like going to the movies.
You get up afterward
and go out
saying, how was it?
Tell me, tell me how was it.

THE APPARITION

True to his word, our vet
comes in late afternoon
and kneels in a slant of sun.
A pat, a needle stick
stills the failing heart.

We lower the ancient form
to the hemlock-shrouded grave
and before the hole is brimmed
set a layer of chicken wire
to guard against predators

so that the earth we broke
re-forms, a mild mound.
The rock we place on top
common glacial granite
is mica-flecked and flat.

That night the old dog works
his way back up and out
gasping, salted with dirt
and barks his familiar bark
at the scribble-scratched back door.

I pull on shirt and pants
a Pavlovian response
and stumble half awake
downstairs to turn the knob
where something, some mortal stub

I swear I recognize:
some flap of ear or fur
swims out of nothingness
and brushes past me
into its rightful house.

WOMEN AND HORSES

After Auschwitz, to write a poem is barbaric.
　　　　　　　　—Theodor Adorno

After Auschwitz: after ten of my father's kin—
the ones who stayed—starved, then were gassed in the camps.
After Vietnam, after Korea, Kuwait, Somalia, Haiti, Afghanistan.
After the Towers. This late in the life of our haplessly orbiting world
let us celebrate whatever scraps the muse, that naked child,
can pluck from the still-smoldering dumps.

If there's a lyre around, strike it! A body, stand back, give it air!
Let us have sparrows laying their eggs in bluebird boxes.
Let us have bluebirds insouciantly nesting elsewhere.
Lend us navel-bared teens, eyebrow- and nose-ringed prodigies
crumbling breakfast bagels over dog-eared and jelly-smeared texts.
Allow the able-bodied among us to have steamy sex.

Let there be fat old ladies in flowery tent dresses at bridge tables.
Howling babies in dirty diapers and babies serenely at rest.
War and détente will go on, détente and renewed tearings asunder,
we can never break free from the dark and degrading past.
Let us see life again, nevertheless, in the words of Isaac Babel
as a meadow over which women and horses wander.

JACK

How pleasant the yellow butter
melting on white kernels, the meniscus
of red wine that coats the insides of our goblets

where we sit with sturdy friends as old as we are
after shucking the garden's last Silver Queen
and setting husks and stalks aside for the horses

the last two of our lives, still noble to look upon:
our first foal, now a bossy mare of 28
which calibrates to 84 in people years

and my chestnut gelding, not exactly a youngster
at 22. Every year, the end of summer
lazy and golden, invites grief and regret:

suddenly it's 1980, winter batters us,
winds strike like cruelty out of Dickens. Somehow
we have seven horses for six stalls. One of them,

a big-nosed roan gelding, calm as a president's portrait
lives in the rectangle that leads to the stalls. We call it
the motel lobby. Wise old campaigner, he dunks his

hay in the water bucket to soften it, then visits the others
who hang their heads over their Dutch doors. Sometimes
he sprawls out flat to nap in his commodious quarters.

That spring, in the bustle of grooming
and riding and shoeing, I remember I let him go
to a neighbor I thought was a friend, and the following

fall she sold him down the river. I meant to
but never did go looking for him, to buy him back
and now my old guilt is flooding this twilit table

my guilt is ghosting the candles that pale us to skeletons
the ones we must all become in an as yet unspecified order.
Oh Jack, tethered in what rough stall alone

did you remember that one good winter?

WHICH ONE

I eye the driver of the Chevrolet
pulsing beside me at a traffic light

the chrome-haired woman in the checkout line
chatting up the acned clerk

the clot of kids smoking on the sly
in the Mile-Hi Pizza parking lot

the meter reader, the roofer at work
next door, a senior citizen

stabbing the sidewalk with his three-pronged cane.
Which one of you discarded in a bag

—sealed with duct tape—in the middle of the road
three puppies four or five weeks old

who flung two kittens from a moving car
at midnight into a snowbank where

the person trailing you observed the leg
and tail of the calico one that lived

and if not you, someone flossing her teeth
or watering his lawn across the street.

I look for you wherever I go.

THE JEW ORDER

Mr. Welchon was a dusty, disappointed man.
He taught American History to my tenth-grade class
and was famous for his stringent pop quizzes.
The points of his shirt collars splayed out unhappily
on either side of his fat ties. Not a single girl
in the room had a crush on him.

This was an upscale high school in the suburbs
at a time when men wore suits and women skirts below the knee.
Because my mother was ambitious for me, I commuted
on two trolleys, an hour each way. Half of
the student body was Jewish, a quarter black.
The football team was salt and pepper, heavy on the pepper.

We yawned our way through the Civil War
the dates of battles, the burning of Atlanta
Sherman's march to the sea, the one black regiment
that fought on the Union side, the surrender at Appomattox.
Ulysses S. Grant, a splendid classical name. We knew
he drank too much, that fact was in the history book

but not the Jew Order that he issued
out of Oxford, Mississippi, in 1862
expelling all Jews as a class from Union territory
in the Ohio and Mississippi valleys
within 24 hours of receipt of this command
for violating every regulation of trade.

Had we talked about how few Jews lived then
in the South, most of them merchants and traders
some of them daring to smuggle cotton up North
to bring in flour or shoes, salt or medicine
for the desperate Confederate households
risking death by hanging to slip past the blockade

had we heard, for example, of the woman in Richmond
before their dodgy shipments, being charged
$70 for a barrel of flour, who exclaimed, *My God!*
I have seven children! How am I to feed them all?
to whom the shopkeeper replied, *I do not know, Madam,*
unless you eat your children; young as we were

had we read further that any Jews who remained
would be held in confinement as prisoners
except that Morris Hoffman of St. Louis together
with his little cluster of B'nai B'rith brothers
threw themselves *on the bosom of our father, Abraham*
in the name of religious liberty and justice

asking him to annul that order and protect his
humblest constituents, wouldn't we have looked
at one another? Wouldn't we have felt the smallest spasm
of national pride when Lincoln said: *This protection*
you shall have? He revoked the Jew decree
the same month he signed the Emancipation.

Young as we were, had we read these two exchanges
wouldn't we have looked at one another
black kids at white and vice versa
sharing our adolescent fury at injustice
our radical innocence, our masturbatory guilt
wouldn't we all have looked at Mr. Welchon

who was there to teach and guide us in his boredom
he at the blackboard at the front of the room
we in our restless alphabetically integrated rows
for calling the roll, wouldn't we all
have looked at one another
with a heady momentary taste of solidarity?

WHERE ANY OF US

Where any of us is
going in tomorrow's reckless Lexus is
the elemental mystery: despite

instructions he left behind, Houdin-
i, who could outwit
ropes and chains, padlocks and steam-

er trunks, could extricate
himself from underwater metal crates,
could send forth, he was certain,

a message from the other side,
never cracked the curtain
and Mary Baker Eddy's telephone

said to be hooked up in her crypt—
would it have been
innocence or arrogance,

such trust in the beyond?—
has, mythic, failed to ring. If
they knew the script

these two (God may be love
or not) they left, tightlipped
and unfulfilled.

As we will.

THE BURNERS, THE BURIERS

Everything I leave behind me, burn unread
wrote Kafka to Max Brod.

Petrarch consigned a thousand
worksheets, he said, *to Vulcan for correction*

and Henry James in a fit of depression
burned his correspondence with

the magisterial Edith.
We might have lost

the whole *Aeneid* had Augustus
not overridden Virgil's

deathbed request. Plato as well
mistrusting his *2nd Epistle*

declared
it should be set afire

but Alexander Pope asked everyone
to send his letters back again

so he could elaborate upon them
for publication.

When Prussian soldiers threatened
to storm the gates in 1871

Flaubert burned what was thought to be
a packet from Louise Colet

and far too hastily
Dante Gabriel Rossetti

griefstricken when
she overdosed on laudanum

buried all his yet
unpublished oeuvre with wife Elizabeth.

Seven years elapsed until
his want overtook his will.

Good friends then exhumed
his manuscript from her grisly room.

But it was the Russian poets who
knew how to dig a hole for, take a match to

hoard paper, make do
with scratches on a bar of soap

who smuggled out, besmirched and pied
their Cyrillics of rage and hope

excoriating lines we weep to read
yet leave them no less dead

Osip Mandelstam
sentenced for his Stalin epigram

Vasil Stus
buried with other *zeks*

along the Potma rail line
assigned a stone with number but no name.

So little rescued for posterity:
Everything I leave behind me, hold fast. Keep dry.

ON BEING ASKED DURING A NATIONAL CRISIS TO WRITE A POEM IN CELEBRATION OF THE BICENTENNIAL OF RALPH WALDO EMERSON

Caught up in a metaphorical swoon
by the oversoul in his head
War is on its last legs, he said.
The question is only How Soon.
Swayed by the cradling springs of his bed-
rock trust in the final perfec-
tibility of man, he elec-
ted Nature and found Her good.
This week a hunter sighting his gun
on a flock of ducks at that sacramental
hour when waterfowl season opens
said *pulling the trigger is transcendental.*

ODE

Upside down and backward
windmilling through
sometimes satin sometimes

sullen murk, sun a tatted doily
intercut by overhanging pines
and hemlock, gliding

not too close to either
shore, water flowing
in and out of me

as I scoop deep
behind me, stroke
scoop and fling hands'-sprayfuls

straight-armed again and again
I salute you, Eleanor,
who outswam them all back-

stroking left right
somersault touch push off,
churning to the Olympic gold in 1932

ELEANOR HOLM
kicked off the team
in 1936 for drinking champagne

and shooting craps
in the first-class lounge with
Helen Hayes

aboard the SS *Manhattan*
I say ENCORE!
I raise a glass to you, Eleanor.

THE ZEN OF MOWING

How well I know
the litany of my long afternoon, the engine's lulling drone
that slithers

under my earmuffs
as I glide on its steadfast thrum. How exactly I set the
mower's inner wheel

so that it overlaps
the wavery lush first swipe I've cut across this late-September
meadow

humped with
granite outcrops. The newly sharpened blade takes down
milkweed, mullein,

thistle, purple
clover, Indian paintbrush, nettle, ragweed, late-summer asters,
orchard

grass, timothy
in an effortless pass punctuated by an occasional stutter when
the machine

encounters the
stubble of last year's sumac forcing a new tree up on the
insistent root

of the old, for
even after the blade has severed them, every switch-like stalk
is engaged

underground in
regrouping thread by thread, going on as we do, fiercely but
soundlessly.

I look back.
I see not where I am going but where I have been. The
stripes of my hard-

won greensward salute me. I sink into my zen.

FOR STANLEY, SOME LINES AT RANDOM

You, Sir, with the red snippers
who twice saw Halley's comet fly,
you, who can identify
Coprinus, chanterelle and sundry
others of the damp-woods fleet,
whose broadside "The Long Boat"
produced on handmade paper
woven from your discards—
here, the delivery boy declared
is Mr. Kunitz's laundry—
hangs in my study,

it's forty years since I, a guest
in your Provincetown retreat
arose from what you said
had once been e. e. cummings's bed
to breakfast on an omelet
fat with choice boletuses
that had erupted in
your three-tiered garden,
perhaps under one of your dahlias
the size of a dinner plate,
a garden that took decades to create.

Luck of the alphabet,
since 1961 we've leaned
against each other, spine
on spine, positioned thus.
Upright or slant, long may we stand
on shelves dusted or not
to be taken up by hands
that cherish us.

SONNET IN SO MANY WORDS

The time comes when it can't be said,
thinks Richard Dalloway, pocketing his
sixpence of change, and off he goes
holding a great bunch of white and red

roses against his chest, thinking himself
a man both blessed and doomed in wedlock
and Clarissa meanwhile thinking as he walks back
even between husband and wife a gulf. . . .

If these are Virginia and Leonard, are they not
also you and me taking up the coffee
grinder or scraping bits of omelet free
for the waiting dogs who salivate and sit?

Never to say what one feels. And yet
this is a love poem. Can you taste it?

STILL TO MOW

MULCHING

Me in my bugproof netted headpiece kneeling
to spread sodden newspapers between broccolis,
corn sprouts, cabbages and four kinds of beans,

prostrate before old suicide bombings, starvation,
AIDS, earthquakes, the unforeseen tsunami,
front-page photographs of lines of people

with everything they own heaped on their heads,
the rich assortment of birds trilling on all
sides of my forest garden, the exhortations

of commencement speakers at local colleges,
the first torture revelations under my palms
and I a helpess citizen of a country

I used to love, who as a child wept when
the brisk police band bugled *Hats off! The flag
is passing by*, now that every wanton deed

in this stack of newsprint is heartbreak,
my blackened fingers can only root in dirt,
turning up industrious earthworms, bits

of unreclaimed eggshell, wanting to ask
the earth to take my unquiet spirit,
bury it deep, make compost of it.

THE DOMESTIC ARRANGEMENT

from Dorothy Wordsworth's journals

Wm went into the wood to alter his poems
writes Dorothy. *I shelled peas, gathered beans,*
and worked in the garden. This is Grasmere

where she picked and boiled gooseberries
two lbs. of sugar in the first panfull
while *Wm went into the wood to alter his poems*

a trip he makes almost daily, composng
the lines she will later copy. Mornings
she works in the garden at Grasmere

which looked so beautiful my heart
almost melted away, she confides
while Wm's in the wood altering his poems.

On one of their daily walks she observes
helpful details of Wm's famed daffodils.
Then it's back to the garden at Grasmere

where she ties up her scarlet runner beans
and pulls a bag of peas for Miss Simpson.
Leave Wm in the wood to alter his poems;
praise Dorothy in the garden at Grasmere.

THE FINAL POEM

Bread Loaf, late August, the chemistry
of a New England fall already
inviting the swamp maples to flare.

Magisterial in the white wicker rocker
Robert Frost at rest after giving
a savage reading

holding nothing back, his rage
at dying, *not yet*, as he barged
his chair forth, then back, *don't sit*

*there mumbling in the shadows, call
yourselves poets?* All
but a handful scattered. Fate

rearranged us happy few at his feet.
He rocked us until midnight. I took
away these close-lipped dicta. *Look*

*up from the page. Pause between poems.
Say something about the next one.
Otherwise the audience*

*will coast, they can't take in
half of what you're giving them.*
Reaching for the knob of his cane

he rose, and flung this exit line:
Make every poem your final poem.

XOCHI'S TALE

Is it my fault I'm part rat terrier, part
the kind of dog who lives in a lady's lap?
I didn't ask to be bottom mutt in the pack
that runs untamed through the twisted trash-strewn streets
in Xochiapulcho, I didn't ask to be plucked
up by a pair of gringos. First, they took
away my manhood. No more sweet reek
of bitches, no hot pursuits, no garbage rot.
When they packed up to go back to the USA
I thought they'd cry, then dump me out, but no.

Macho mestizo, my entry papers say.
Who dines in style and sleeps the sleep of kings
ought dream no more of his rowdy half-starved days. . . .
I dwell in heaven but without the wings.

VIRGIL

He came, a dog auspiciously named Virgil,
homeless, of unknown breed but clearly hound
barking at scents, aroused by hot ones to bugle.
His first week here he brought three squirrels to ground
and lined their mangled corpses up on the grass
to be—why not?—admired before burial.
He gobbled the snottiest tissues from the trash.
Also, he swiped our lunches off the table.
He knew not *sit* or *stay*, has still to take in
that chasing sheep and horses is forbidden.
When reprimanded, he grovels, penitent.
He longs for love with all his poet's soul.
　　His eyebrows make him look intelligent.
　　We save our choicest food scraps for his bowl.

ESSAY, FRESHMAN COMP

A student of mine turned in a composition
about shooting pigeons in his uncle's barn.
He peppered them with beebees.

They just sat there in the rafters
spots of red appearing on their breasts.
Eventually they toppled. The ones

that were still flapping he stomped on.
He says that he was eight or nine, he claims
that kids that age don't know what death is.

He's since become a vegetarian,
a lifetime of expiation ahead of him
in southern Ohio where it's raining

on newly thawed fields and there's a nitrate
alert from all the fertilizer
washing down into the ground water,

contaminating local wells. They say
drinking it is still okay for grownups
though not for kids too young

to know what death is.

THE ZEN OF MUCKING OUT

I never liked this stubbled field so much
as now, Keats wrote John Reynolds
and in my upper pasture I feel the same

where the last two horses of our lives
are at their day-long work reducing
the lightly frosted grass of mid-October

to manure, and I at mine, my five-
foot fork with ten metal tines, the hickory
handle worn down by my grip

so many years it almost seems to sweat—
muck basket to wheelbarrow, fork
upended till I reach the mother bed

and dump my smeary load, then stop.
White pine embroidery to the east,
a narrow view of Pumpkin Hill across,

lissome pond behind me. One late
garter snake sits sunning on an outcrop.
From the highway the vigor of sirens

announces a world of metal and speed
beyond my blinkered allegiance
to this task. My fingerprint,

my footstep. My zen.

PLEASE PAY ATTENTION AS THE ETHICS
HAVE CHANGED

—tagline, New Yorker *cartoon, May 10, 2004*

Four hundred and seventeen pen-raised pheasants
were rattled—think stick

on a picket fence—into flight
for the Vice President's gun. And after that

hundreds of pen-reared mallards
were whooshed

up to be killed
by, among others, a Supreme Court Justice.

Statistics provided by HSUS—
the Humane Society of the United States.

The exact number of ducks, however, is wanting—
this is canned hunting

where you don't stay to pluck
the feathers, pull the innards out. Fuck

all of that. You don't do shit
except shoot.

But where is that other Humane Society, the one with rules
we used to read aloud in school

the one that takes away your license to collar
and leash a naked prisoner

the one that forbids you to sodomize
a detainee before the cold eyes

of your fellow MPs?
When the pixie soldier says cheese

for the camera who says *please pay attention?*
The ethics have changed.

Fuck the Geneva Convention.

EXTRAORDINARY RENDITION

Only the oak and the beech hang onto their leaves
at the end, the oak leaves bruised the color of those
insurgent boys Iraqi policemen captured

purpling their eyes and cheekbones before
lining them up to testify to the Americans
that, no, no, they had not been beaten. . . .

The beech leaves dry to brown, a palette of cinnamon.
They curl undefended, they have no stake in the outcome.
Art redeems us from time, it has been written.

Meanwhile we've exported stress positions, shackles,
dog attacks, sleep deprivation, waterboarding.
To rend: *to tear (one's garments or hair)*

in anguish or rage. To render: *to give what is due
or owed.* The Pope's message
this Sunday is the spiritual value of suffering.

Extraordinary how the sun comes up
with its rendition of daybreak,
staining the sky with indifference.

ENTERING HOUSES AT NIGHT

None of us spoke their language and
none of them spoke ours.
We went in breaking down doors.

They told us to force the whole scrum
—men women kids—into one room.
We went in punching kicking yelling out orders

in our language, not theirs.
The front of one little boy bloomed
wet as we went in breaking down doors.

Now it turns out that 80 percent
of the ones in that sweep were innocent
as we punched kicked yelled out orders.

The way that we spun in that sweltering stink
with handcuffs and blindfolds was rank.
We went in breaking down doors.

Was that the Pyrrhic moment when
we herded the sobbing women with guns
as punching kicking yelling out orders
we went in breaking down doors?

WHAT YOU DO

when nobody's looking
in the black sites what you do
when nobody knows you
are in there what you do

when you're in the black sites
when you shackle them higher
in there what you do
when you kill by crucifixion

when you shackle them higher
are you still Christian
when you kill by crucifixion
when you ice the body

are you still Christian
when you wrap it in plastic
when you ice the body
when you swear it didn't happen

when you wrap it in plastic
when the dossier's been there
when you swear it didn't happen
for over a year now

when the dossier's been there
for the ghost prisoner
for over a year now
where nobody's looking

for the ghost prisoner
when nobody knows what
you do when you're in there
where nobody's looking.

THE BEHEADINGS

The guillotine at least was swift. After
the head pitched sideways into a basket
and was raised to a thirsty crowd that roared
approval of death from above, the sun turned
a garish yellow and froze on the horizon
raying out behind the jellied blood the way
it once stood still over Jericho at Joshua's command
and the day held its breath. . . .

After they sawed through Nicholas Berg's neck
with an inadequate knife while he screamed,
after the heads of Daniel Pearl
and Paul Johnson were detached
in midthought, in terror but
caught alive on a grainy video, what
did their stored oxygen enable them to mouth,
and Kim-Sun-il who danced his last lines
declaiming over and over on worldwide television
I don't want to die what rose from his lips?

It was always night behind the blindfold.
Like bats in midflight at dusk
scrolling their thready messages come
words we can never capture, the soul
perhaps flying out from whatever aperture?
—a pox on belief in the soul!—and yet
there's no denying we are witness to
something more than
involuntary twitching going on

the air filling with fleeing souls
as it did in 1790, and filling again today
this poem a paltry testimony
to the nameless next and next—
Turks, Bulgarians, Filipinos whose heads
—severed, it is said the head retains
several seconds of consciousness—
will roll, reroll as in *revolution*
a time of major crustal deformation
when folds and faults are formed

time enough, in several languages
to recite a prayer, compose a grocery list
as the day holds its breath.

REVISIONIST HISTORY:
THE BRITISH UGANDA PROGRAM OF 1903

A paradise in Africa?
How generous of the British
to offer a new Jerusalem
to the conference of Zionists,

an ample chunk of fertile land
to plow and plant, that the wandering
Jews might wander no more.

Dispatched, the three-man delegation
returned wild-eyed with tales
of lions, leopards, elephants
roaming the yellow veldt at will.

Also a warrior tribe, the Masai,
handsome as statues, whose cattle, given
to them by God, are their Torah.

In the words of Theodor Herzl:
The natives are to be gently
persuaded to move to other lands.
So far, this is history.

     But what if the Masai,
     proud lion hunters, laid down
     their spears, became willing partners?

First a trickle, then a torrent.
They came with wheelbarrows, seeds and hoes.
The proud Masai helped gather cow patties,
watched as these Jewish blacksmiths and tailors

devoutly turned them under the soil,
watched as grasslands gave way to gardens
heavy with peas, cabbages, melon.

> What if the Jews grew browner,
> the Masai grew paler until
> the plateau was all café au lait?

To fatten the cattle the Jews raised alfalfa.
The Tribe of Masai ate eggplants and greens.
They blessed each other's Torahs. Amen.
The wandering Jews wandered no more.

THE SAVING REMNANT

Turn it and turn it
the old rabbis said
for everything is in it
except for the goddess
hatching her world-egg
except for the planet
she births from her navel
my father is in it
lifting his wine cup
breaking the challah
Fridays at sundown
my father declaiming
and it was evening
and it was morning
of the seventh day and
God rested on the seventh
day from all the work that
He had made the war in
Europe not yet started
my three older brothers
still at the table
who will ship out to
Rommel's North Africa
the Hump over Burma
the calm Caribbean
meanwhile my mother's hair
has not yet silvered

she fills the soup bowls
she serves the roast beef
rare at the center
and God saw that it
was good for hadn't He
chosen us from among
all people to survive.

I turn it and turn it
the parents have vanished
taking my brothers
one after another
and it was evening
and it was morning
I speak my own asides
into time's mirror
objects in the mirror
are closer than they appear
the past is as fragrant
as line-dried linens
my father the patriarch
laying the law down
my mother the peacemaker
straddling the yellow line
subversive subservient
nods to the goddess
hatching her world-egg

nods to the planet
she lifts from her navel
meanwhile still dwelling
inside his mother
David recited
a poem a poem
God cut out and saved to
paste in His scrapbook
the one that excludes us
who carry and give birth
who wash up and cover
what could He call it
the saving remnant.

THE IMMUTABLE LAWS

Never buy land on a slope, my father declared
the week before his heart gave out.
We bit down hard on a derelict diary farm
of tilting fields, hills, humps and granite outcrops.

Never bet what you can't afford to lose,
he lectured. I bet my soul on a tortured horse
who never learned to love, but came to trust me.

Spend your money close to where you earn it,
he dictated. Nothing made him crosser
than wives who drove to New York to go shopping
when Philly stores had everything they needed.

This, the grab bag of immutable laws
circa 1940 when I was the last
child left at home to be admonished:

Only borrow what you know you can repay.
Your mother used to run up dress-shop bills
the size of the fifth Liberty Loan,
his private hyperbole. It took me years

to understand there'd been five loans
launched to finance the First World War,
the one he fought in, *the war to end all wars.*

What would this man who owed no man, who kept
his dollars folded in a rubber band,
have thought of credit cards, banking online?
Wars later, clear as water, I hear him say

reconcile your checkbook monthly, and oh!
always carry a clean handkerchief.

THOUGH HE TARRY

I believe with perfect faith in
the coming of the Messiah
and though he tarry I will
wait daily for his coming
said Maimonides in 1190
or so and 44 percent
of people polled in the USA
in 2007 are also waiting
for him to show up in person—
though of course he won't <u>be</u> a person.

Do we want to save our planet,
the only one we know of,
so the faithful 44 percent
can be in a state of high alert
in case he arrives in person
though of course he won't <u>be</u> a person?

According to Stephen Jay Gould
      science and religion are
      non-overlapping magisteria.
      See each elbowing the other
      to shove over on the bed
      they're condemned to share?
      See how they despise, shrink back
      from accidental touching?

It's no surprise that
60 percent of scientists
say they are nonbelievers.

But whether you're churchy or not
what about the planet?
Damn all of you with dumpsters.
Damn all who do not compost.
Damn all who tie their dogs out
on bare ground, without water.
Damn all who debeak chickens
and all who eat them, damn
CEOs with bonuses,
corporate jets, trophy wives.

Damn venal human nature
lurching our way to a sorry
and probably fiery finale. . . .
If only he'd strap his angel wings on
in the ether and get his licensed
and guaranteed ass down here—
though of course he won't <u>be</u> a person—
if only he wouldn't tarry.

WHEN THE MESSIAH COMES

The first green pushing past the last snow,
the old horses in their spattered coats of rubbed plush
lined up facing downhill, sunbathing,
shedding great handfuls of hair toward the reckoning
when the Messiah comes up the sluicy drive
and the crows, holding nothing back,
halloo their praise.

ASCENDING

The grapes just forming are green beads
as tight on the stalk as if hammered into place,
the swelling unripe juveniles are almost
burgundy, promising yet withholding
and the ones they have come for, the highest
blue-black clusters wearing a dusting of white,
veiled dancers, tantalize in the wind.
Wrens weaving in and out, small bugs, pale sun.
Two bony old people in the back forty,
one holding the ladder, one ascending.

LOOKING BACK IN MY EIGHTY-FIRST YEAR

How did we get to be old ladies—
my grandmother's job—when we
were the long-leggèd girls?
—Hilma Wolitzer

Instead of marrying the day after graduation,
in spite of freezing on my father's arm as
here comes the bride struck up,
saying, I'm not sure I want to do this,

I should have taken that fellowship
to the University of Grenoble to examine
the original manuscript
of Stendhal's unfinished *Lucien Leuwen*,

I, who had never been west of the Mississippi,
should have crossed the ocean
in third class on the Cunard White Star,
the war just over, the Second World War

when Kilroy was here, that innocent graffito,
two eyes and a nose draped over
a fence line. How could I go?
Passion had locked us together.

Sixty years my lover,
he says he would have waited.
He says he would have sat
where the steamship docked

till the last of the pursers
decamped, and I rushed back
littering the runway with carbon paper. . . .
Why didn't I go? It was fated.

Marriage dizzied us. Hand over hand,
flesh against flesh for the final haul,
we tugged our lifeline through limestone and sand,
lover and long-leggèd girl.

DURING THE ASSASSINATIONS

I took the cello to its lesson,
the cheerleader to the gym.
I was a sixties soccer mom

and when the bassoon needed
double reeds to suck on
I scoured Boston.

I bought red knee-highs for the cheerleader.
Skirts wide enough to straddle
the cello onstage.

Cacophony of warm-up, then
the oboe's A, *every*
good boy does fine, football

games with fake pompoms
siss-boom-ba and after,
gropings under the grandstands.

I went where I was called to go.
I clapped, I comforted.
I kept my eyes on Huntley and Brinkley.

During the assassinations
I marched with other soccer moms.
I carried lemons in case of tear gas.

I have a dream became my dream.
I stood all night
on the steps of the Pentagon.

With each new death
I added my grief
to the grief of millions

but always her pink suit
on the flat trunk of the limousine
and in her hand a piece of his skull.

THE LOWER CHESAPEAKE BAY

Whatever happened to the cross-chest carry,
the head carry, the hair carry,

the tired-swimmer-put-your-hands-on-my-shoulders-
and-look-in-my-eyes retrieval, and what

became of the stride jump when you leap
from impossible heights and land with your head

above water so that you never lose sight
of your drowning person, or if he is close enough, where

is the lifesaver ring attached to a rope
you can hurl at your quarry, then haul

him to safety, or as a last resort
where is the dock onto which you tug

the unconscious soul, place him facedown,
clear his mouth, straddle his legs and press

with your hands on both sides of his rib cage
to the rhythm of *out goes the bad air in*

comes the good and pray he will breathe,
hallowed methods we practiced over and over

the summer I turned eighteen to win
my Water Safety Instructor's badge

and where is the boy from Ephrata, PA
I made out with night after night in the lee

of the rotting boathouse at a small dank camp
on the lower Chesapeake Bay?

PERSPECTIVE

First learn perspective, Leonardo said
then draw from nature.

Stubbs's *Whistlejacket* answers
on a canvas nine feet tall

commissioned in 1762
by the Second Marquess of Rockingham.

This horse looks out
at any who look in, looks out

prickeared, exaggerated mane and tail
caught in a half-levade, hocks over heels.

O horse of my heart, hang on at this still point
as all around us open-air markets explode,

body parts rain down and families
rush to collect them, else no afterlife.

The priest insists that animals are sinless,
have no souls, won't appear in heaven,

his heaven, not the paradise
of expectant virgins. Where

Whistlejacket went is
not revealed, into the ground,

perhaps, in his final pasture,
O horse of my heart, full nine feet tall.

THE CORSET SHOP

The heavy oak door of Madame Marguerite's corseterie
at a good address in downtown Philly

circa 1932, opens onto such pink
such rosy froufrou that the enchanted child thinks

she has wandered into a candy store.
Madame and her mother air-kiss three times while the armor

of their torsos cannot avoid making
contact with a small click. Her mother has come for a fitting.

Madame is so eager she glistens.
Business has slowed to a trickle. This is the Depression.

The child is shown to an armchair
that swallows her. She dozes in the perfumed air.

In the backroom a slavey bends over
a sewing machine stitching, reshaping, repairing. Her love

child, now three or four, plays on the floor with a doll.
This is all the incurious child can recall.

•

Each morning the child I am in this story watches transfixed
as her mother dresses in the shadow of her closet.

She works her way into the brittle frame that encloses
her body from waist-bulge to pubis

then bends forward, inviting her breasts, those floppy spaniel's ears
to slip into place in the brassière

that attaches with small hooks to the corset.
This is before I have breasts, or even a discernible waist.

My body is a smooth column
except for my shoulders; swimming has enhanced them

for I raced in the Y's events from the time I was nine
to my mother's despair. She does not attend.

And my long pigtails are always wet, smelling of chlorine,
ruining the family supper, or so she claims.

Pigtails that I am to hack off with a scissors
three years later. We wrangle over

them endlessly before each morning's redo:
Hold still! Your part is as crooked as Ridge Avenue.

•

I've just had my first period. I have come with my mother
to be fitted by Madame for a brassière.

There is nothing in stock broad enough to stretch
across my back, yet small enough to cup my just emerging breasts.

An item will have to be custom made. The two women giggle
over my barely engorged chest, my flat pink nipples.

Unforgivable, unforgettable, this scene.
I try to expunge it from my memory's screen

as the shop itself disappears,
the old neighborhood falls into disrepair

and Madame, nearly blind and by now quite deaf, totters
about the modest home of her daughter.

·

Now she is gone, let us remember my mother
in hat and gloves, in silk stockings, with appropriate purse no matter

the day's heat or cold, dressed as a lady dresses. Let us stop
on the disreputable daughter, braless behind some shapeless top

holding her mother's note.
I loved seeing you, it said in a tiny cramped script

that wandered downhill on the page. *Even though it was so brief
I loved . . .* The stroke that took her life

came on as gently as a Wedgwood pitcher might pour milk.
She died as she had often requested, in her sleep, uncorseted,
   but in silk.

DEATH, ETC.

I have lived my whole life with death, said William Maxwell,
aetat ninety-one, and haven't we all. Amen to that.
It's all right to gutter out like a candle but the odds are better

for succumbing to a stroke or pancreatic cancer.
I'm not being gloomy, this bright September
when everything around me shines with being:

hummingbirds still raptured in the jewelweed,
puffballs humping up out of the forest duff
and the whole voluptuous garden still putting forth

bright yellow pole beans, deep-pleated purple cauliflowers,
to say nothing of regal white corn that feeds us
night after gluttonous night, with a slobber of butter.

Still, Maxwell's pronouncement speaks to my body's core,
this old body I trouble to keep up the way
I keep up my two old horses, wiping insect deterrent

on their ears, cleaning the corners of their eyes,
spraying their legs to defeat the gnats, currying burrs
out of their thickening coats. They go on grazing thoughtlessly

while winter is gathering in the wings. But it is not given
to us to travel blindly, all the pasture bars down,
to seek out the juiciest grasses, nor to predict

which of these two will predecease the other or to anticipate
the desperate whinnies for the missing that will ensue.
Which of us will go down first is also not given,

a subject that hangs unspoken between us
as with Jocasta, who begs Oedipus not to inquire further.
Meanwhile, it is pleasant to share opinions and mealtimes,

to swim together daily, I with my long slow back and forths,
he with his hundred freestyle strokes that wind him alarmingly.
A sinker, he would drown if he did not flail like this.

We have put behind us the State Department tour
of Egypt, Israel, Thailand, Japan that ended badly
as we leapt down the yellow chutes to safety after a botched takeoff.

We have been made at home in Belgium, Holland, and Switzerland,
narrow, xenophobic Switzerland of clean bathrooms and much butter.
We have travelled by Tube and Métro *in the realms of gold*

paid obeisance to the Winged Victory and the dreaded Tower,
but now it is time to settle as the earth itself settles
in season, exhaling, dozing a little before the fall rains come.

Every August when the family gathers, we pose
under the ancient willow for a series of snapshots,
the same willow, its lumpish trunk sheathed in winking aluminum

that so perplexed us forty years ago, before we understood
the voracity of porcupines. Now hollowed by age and marauders,
its aluminum girdle painted dull brown, it is still leafing

out at the top, still housing a tumult of goldfinches. We try to
hold still
and smile, squinting into the brilliance, the middle-aged chil-
dren,
the grown grandsons, the dogs of each era, always a pair

of grinning shelter dogs whose long lives are but as grasshoppers
compared to our own. We try to live gracefully
and at peace with our imagined deaths but in truth we go for-
ward

stumbling, afraid of the dark,
of the cold, and of the great overwhelming
loneliness of being last.

NOTES

"Credo": I am indebted to N. Scott Momaday, whose retelling of the Indian legend in *The Ancient Child* (Doubleday, 1989) sparked this elaboration.

"The Nuns of Childhood: Two Views": With thanks to Joseph Parisi, whose harsh parochial school memories evoked my nostalgic ones.

"Remarkable Women: An Apostrophe": The magpie in me has drawn on three disparate sources for this poem, from Timothy Foote's article on Potter in *Smithsonian*, "A Tale of Some Tails and the Story of Their Shy Creator," January 1989; Louisa May Alcott's own *Selected Letters* (Little, Brown, 1987); and Donald McCaig's article in *Country Journal*, "Helen Nearing: The Good Life Lived with America's Premier Homesteader," January/February 1990.

"The Rendezvous": Alec Wilkinson's absorbing article on the Tlingits of Admiralty Island (*The New Yorker*, November 26, 1990) gave rise to this poem.

THE LONG MARRIAGE

"The Long Marriage": I am indebted to Bernard F. Scholz, Professor of Comparative Literature, Rijks Universiteit, Groningen, Netherlands, for providing the derivation of the word *torschlusspanik*: it "refers to the rush in and out just before the city gates were closed in the walled towns of the pricipalities which dotted Germany until Napoleon put an end to the 'Kleinstaaterei.'"

JACK AND OTHER NEW POEMS

"New Hampshire, February 7, 2003": A blizzard that many came to call the Storm of the Century struck on this day in 1978. Much of the East Coast was paralyzed; New England was pounded with high winds for two days. Snowdrifts as high as fifteen feet were recorded and fifty-four people died.

"The Jew Order": I am indebted to Amina Sanchez of the Skirball Museum, Los Angeles, for supplying the exact wordage of Grant's decree.

STILL TO MOW

The material in "Entering Houses at Night" is taken from a young female Iraqi's blog dated February 11, 2006, written under the pseudonym Riverbend.

The material in "What You Do" is taken from "A Deadly Interrogation," by Jane Mayer, *The New Yorker*, November 14, 2005.

A sidebar to "Revisionist History: The British Uganda Program of 1903": In 1902, Joseph Chamberlain, British Colonial Secretary, offered five thousand square miles in the British Protectorate as a national homeland for the Jews in what was then designated Uganda. After fierce debate in 1903, the Zionist Congress agreed to send a group to inspect the land and in 1905 politely declined the offer.

ACKNOWLEDGMENTS

Grateful thanks to the editors of the publications in which the poems in New Poems, section I, first appeared, sometimes in slightly different forms: *The Alaska Quarterly Review, The American Poetry Review, The Atlantic, Cavalier Magazine, The Georgia Review, Great River Review, Hudson Review, Margie Review, The Massachussetts Review, New Letters, Per Contra, Ploughshares, Prairie Schooner, The Progressive, St. Petersburg Review.*